Secrets of a
CHAMPION
Student-Athlete

Secrets of a
CHAMPION
Student-Athlete

A Reality Check

OBADELE THOMPSON

Brown Books Publishing Group
Dallas, Texas

Secrets of a Champion Student-Athlete:
A Reality Check
© 2010 Obadele Thompson

Manufactured in the United States of America

For information please contact:
Brown Books Publishing Group
16200 North Dallas Parkway, Suite 170
Dallas, Texas 75248
www.brownbooks.com
(972) 381-0009

A New Era in Publishing™

ISBN-13: 978-1-934812-75-4
ISBN-10: 1-934812-75-7

LCCN: 2010930341
10 9 8 7 6 5 4 3 2 1

To my parents for setting the bar high and, more importantly, for teaching and encouraging me to go higher.

Contents

Preface

It's been a while since I last suited up in my school's colors to compete. I'll admit that some days I look at my college uniform and wish that I could turn back the clock and do it over again. Being a college student-athlete was one of the most valuable and tremendous experiences in my life, one that I would never trade. However, if I had known then what I know now, I certainly would have made some better choices and accomplished so much more than I did. While writing this book, I spoke with several other former student-athletes, including some past NCAA champions, and I realized that I was not alone in feeling this way.

Relatively few student-athletes will stand on the top of the podium in their sport or finish college with an overall 4.0 GPA. Those are great achievements, but being a champion student-athlete is so much more than hoisting a winner's trophy or graduating at the top of your class. It's about overcoming personal obstacles, pushing yourself to new heights, recovering from failures and disappointments, and making the most of your opportunities before your eligibility ends.

Much has changed in college sports since my last collegiate competition, but what it takes to become a champion student-athlete is very much the same, whether you are a walk-on or a scholarship athlete. Although most of the stories in this book are about me, this book is not really about me. My time as a student-athlete is over; now's your time to shine—this book is for you.

Many things in this book will sound familiar to you because you've probably already heard them from your parents, your coaches, and your professors, including setting goals, working hard, and managing your time properly. In addition to these well-known bits of advice and common sense, this book offers a wide range of practical tips and reality checks for you to consider and apply to your daily life as a student-athlete. Most of these "secrets" are the same ones that helped me to excel as a student-athlete and to become an Olympic medalist during the course of my decade-long career as a professional athlete. I also added some bonus "secrets" that can help you gain an edge in your college experience that I wish I had known or practiced when I was a student-athlete.

There are no shortcuts to success. However, I hope that in some way this book can help you to reach your personal goals and potential sooner and easier, so you too can become a champion in the classroom, on the field, and, most importantly, in life.

Acknowledgments

Many have directly and indirectly made contributions to this book, and I thank them all. I especially want to mention a few whose hard work and input allowed my ideas and passion for this book to become a reality.

Foremost, I would like to thank God for the strength and wisdom to complete this task.

To Marion and our kids, thanks for your loving encouragement, understanding, and sacrifices, particularly during my many late night, library, and bookstore writing sessions. I love you and owe you all greatly.

Special thanks to my parents, Dr. Alvin and Hilda Thompson, and family for their constant support and advice throughout this journey. I could not have finished without you.

Rich Nichols' legal and editorial input was invaluable. He believed in the project from the start and went the extra mile on so many occasions to help make it all come together. I am indebted to Kenny Hansmire, who after hearing Rich's outline for the book—before even meeting me—immediately gave his blessing and support to the project.

The staff at Brown Books Publishing deserves much praise, especially, Milli Brown, for her professional yet personal touch, and Janet Harris, whose patience and instruction throughout the process constantly challenged me to improve as a writer.

(Even now I can still hear her telling me to "write tight.") Also, I thank Dena Hill, whose skillful editing brought a needed focus to my manuscript. (I know it wasn't always easy.)

Special thanks to my college coach, Robert "Bob" Kitchens, for his straightforward feedback, which, as usual, was timely and accurate.

I thank those whose ideas, comments, and feedback have in some way shaped this book. Special thanks to Sue Humphrey, Bavu Blakes, Andrea Blackett, Jason St. Hill, Rohan Gilkes, Melissa Johnson, Kareem and Jackie Streete-Thompson, Curtis Hollomon, Lisa Campos, David Brokaw, Kenneth Schropshire, Henry McKoy, Ross Bomben, Frank Miller Jr., Lemar Seale, Eric Frempong, Terrence Trammell, and Victor Houston. Thanks to Carter Love for the portraits and to Jaime Schwaberow and Michael Dickson from Richard Clarkson and Associates, LLC., for assisting me in securing the rights for the NCAA photos. Additionally, I would like to thank Dr. Diana Natalicio, President, The University of Texas-El Paso (UTEP), for her support and advice and coach Mike Krzyzewki for his gracious endorsement.

Finally, my appreciation also goes out to so many others whose roles in life, especially during college, helped me to grow and succeed. These include my former coaches, teammates, trainers, professors, classmates, mentors, friends, supporters, and even competitors. Thank you all.

CHEAT SHEET:
10 TIPS TO REMEMBER WHEN READING THIS BOOK

1. Read with the aim to learn and to improve. You'll get far more from this book when you read with purpose.

2. Look for the main point of stories, reality checks, tips, and "secrets." Use your thinking cap.

3. Read with an open mind. Think honestly about how whatever is discussed relates to your life now and to what you want to achieve.

4. Keep a pencil, pen, or highlighter handy so you can quickly come back to whatever challenges, motivates, or confuses you.

5. Think of this book as being similar to your season. The beginning chapters are like preseason training, full of the basics and the not-always-so-fun but important stuff. Later chapters build on these fundamentals and offer many more practical day-to-day tips.

6. You don't have to read it cover to cover in one sitting. In fact, reading it over multiple sittings may help you to understand and absorb the book better.

7. Read it during your downtime, such as when you are on road trips, during holidays, on the weekend, when you have free time, or when you need something to motivate you.

8. Try to answer the "One-On-One" questions at the end of each chapter.

9. Whatever you learn, try to apply it to your life and to share it with others.

10. This book is just a template and blueprint for success, not a shortcut or a way for you to avoid doing hard work.

1

START STRONG

There I stood, at the starting line, my heart racing with anticipation. Not only was I moments away from the start of one of the marquee match-ups of the Championships, I was also moments away from the final race of my collegiate career—I was a senior. If I succeeded in winning this race, I would become one of few athletes in NCAA Division I track and field history to win both the 100- and 200-meter dashes at the same National Championships. If I failed, I would end my collegiate career with a loss. The stakes were high.

There he stood, only feet away in the outside lane next to me, ready to stop me from winning this elusive NCAA Outdoor 200-meter dash title. He was hungry to win his first NCAA Championships title; I was hungry to end my career by winning my fourth one. Our journeys to this point were different, but we shared a singular, consuming goal—to win! Although I had won the 100-meter dash title in the driving rain about an hour before, that had done little to calm my nerves.

1

I had entered that race as the favorite because, frankly, he had chosen to skip that event despite having the best time in the nation and recently defeating me. Even though I was a two-time NCAA Indoor 200-meter dash champion, he had entered this race as the favorite because of his superior time and win-loss record against me that season. Only two weekends before, he had impressively beaten me at our Outdoor Conference Championships. Once again, our paths had collided, and once more, only one of us could emerge as the champion.

When the starter called us to our marks, a hush moved across the stadium. In that instant, my mind quickly flashed back through my collegiate career. Suddenly, all the hard work I had put in, the sacrifices I had made, the lessons I had learned, and the experiences that I had been through in the last four years flooded my mind. How quickly those four years had passed! I could still vividly remember my first day on campus. Now, in just about 20 seconds of running, my collegiate career would be over.

This is it, I thought to myself. *Showtime!* I positioned myself in the starting blocks and waited for the starter's next command.

"Set!" I assumed the set position. My muscles flexed, and my mind momentarily went blank, ready to react to the next sound.

Moments later, the starter's gun cracked, and I exploded out of the blocks fully focused on executing and committed to winning. I was in a "zone." I caught everyone by the end of the turn, and I continued to drive on into the straightaway, through the rain, through the headwinds, and through the pain. My arms and legs continued working vigorously in perfect harmony as the pitter-patter of my feet on the wet track became my only companion. It was no longer about revenge, rivalries, or redemption. It was about me ending my collegiate career the same way I had begun it four years ago—pushing to reach my potential. At about ten meters from the finish line, I relaxed and raised both my arms in victory. I had finally done it! I had created history and recorded a new personal best in the process.

There I stood, six months later, as the school's banner bearer at my commencement ceremony. When they finally announced my name, I crossed the stage to receive my college degree feeling immensely proud—and relieved—to reach the end of such an important journey in my life.

There I stood, one month later, as a recipient of one of the NCAA's most prestigious awards for student-athletes, the NCAA Today's Top VIII Award. As I crossed the stage to receive my plaque, I felt both proud and humbled to have been selected with the seven other awardees there. They were some of the most accomplished and talented student-athletes of my time, including Peyton Manning from the University of Tennessee, future NFL MVP and Super Bowl Champion.

Even though I was ambitious at the start of my college career, I had no idea that I would have experienced such amazing life moments or become so successful. However, over the next four years of being a student-athlete I learned and practiced certain "secrets" that allowed me to do well in the classroom and on the field, and to be involved in my community. I will share many of these "secrets" with you in this book, but first, let's go over some basics so that you can start strong.

PREPARE FOR CHANGES

When I first came to college, I left all my family and friends behind in Barbados, almost three thousand miles away. I knew this change would challenge me since it meant starting over in an entirely new community and new country. I moved from a small Caribbean island to one of the twenty-five largest cities in the US. Instead of being able to look at the sun set over the beautiful ocean from my home, for four years mountainous desert dominated the view from my dorm room. These changes were only the tip of the iceberg.

Even though I felt confident and focused about what I wanted to do, I was still really unsure and naïve about many things for good reason—college is *not* high school. Fortunately, I had a great support system of family and friends, but they were not physically there to guide, protect, and encourage me through this new experience.

Perhaps my first reality check in college was accepting that I was no longer at home. Although I missed home very much, I had to figure out how to deal with the natural longing to be with my family and friends, especially when I felt lonely and during tougher days because I noticed how those feelings started to overwhelm me and cause me to lose focus on what I needed to do. It wasn't easy, but I learned how to be "present" while I was at school by consciously stopping myself from comparing my home life to my new college life. Also, instead of allowing myself to become too down at being so far away from home, I decided to use my situation as motivation to make the best of my opportunities so that I could make my family and friends proud of me.

Looking back, I realize that besides my family, the coaches, teammates, friends, and mentors who gave me reality checks when I strayed too far from my responsibilities and potential helped me greatly. They showed me how to avoid or navigate situations that could have significantly changed how successful I was as a student-athlete and the course of my life. I came to college as a talented but inexperienced seventeen-year-old and left four years later as a better student, a better athlete, and a more mature person. This journey was not straightforward, however. Along the way, I had to deal with stress, drama, insecurities, misconceptions, ups and downs, and countless changes—some of which I handled better than others.

Like me, all college student-athletes experience a period of transition or starting over on some level regardless of the differences in their backgrounds. For you, it might be moving to a big city from a small town or traveling across the country for school. It might mean taking on a new set of responsibilities like managing your own money, cooking and doing laundry for yourself, having a stranger as a roommate, and, of course, dealing with new coaches and teammates.

REALITY CHECK:
If you're not prepared to change some things in your life, then you won't do well as a college student-athlete.

Throughout college, you will meet people who look, talk, behave, and think differently from you. You may be exposed to new and different climates, cultures, manners, religious and political beliefs, ethnicities, and languages. You will also likely face various challenges at every turn. How you deal with this constant oncoming traffic in your life will determine your fate as a student-athlete. If you are fortunate, you will have people throughout your career who tell you the truth, remind you of the consequences of your choices, and always see more possibilities in your future than you do. Even if you don't have such people in your life, this book is full of reality checks and tips for you to make the most of your time as a student-athlete.

For example, this book will help you learn to look out for and to handle important matters such as successfully discerning the difference between the activities you "need" to do and those you "want" to do. You will also examine more closely who you are and decide what you should hold on to, what you should discard, and what you need to change in your life. In many ways, this book helps you develop the ability to be your own reality check as a student-athlete and beyond.

Your college years provide a training ground on many levels and offer a unique time in your life to make "socially acceptable" mistakes—because you are young. When you leave college, that window of social forgiveness closes quickly, and society will expect you to conduct yourself fully as an adult. In other words, now is your time to explore who you are, learn the rules of the "game," develop your own game plan for success, and prepare for life after college.

Millions of people dream about competing in collegiate athletics, but relatively few experience this special privilege. Regardless of the school you attend, your athletic ability, whether you receive financial aid, or how many victories you amass in your career, never lose sight of the great opportunity that you have right now to wear your school's colors and play collegiate sports.

As a college student-athlete, you are part of one of the largest "fraternities" in the US, comprised of past and present collegiate athletes, both male and female. It boasts some of the greatest athletes, leaders, and people in history. Hopefully, your college experience will be a springboard for great things in your life, whatever you eventually do.

In the United States, more than 400.000 student-athletes compete annually in collegiate athletics, governed mainly by the National Collegiate Athletic Association (NCAA), National Association of Intercollegiate Athletics (NAIA), or National Junior College Athletic Association (NJCAA). All these organizations have long and rich histories, but the NCAA is the biggest and best known of the three. In its three divisions, student-athletes compete in over twenty sports and represent more than a thousand member schools. Our focus will be on the NCAA, although most of the principles covered in this book still apply if you attend a school that is not part of the NCAA.

GET IT STRAIGHT: YOU ARE A STUDENT-ATHLETE

Being a student-athlete is not a valid excuse to lower your expectations or efforts in the classroom or to fulfill negative stereotypes. Contrary to what many believe, gaining a higher education and competing in sports are not mutually exclusive. You can pursue both your academic and athletic goals at a high level and still have time to socialize. I did it, and thousands of other student-athletes do it every year. You don't have to earn an "A" in every course or win every competition, but you should develop the ability to do well in both areas at the same time. The reality checks in this book will help you succeed at both.

In many ways, being both a student and an athlete is like working two demanding jobs, one as a full-time student and the other as a full-time athlete. At some stage, handling all these responsibilities will present a challenge. Most schools spend hundreds of thousands of dollars on resources to help their student-athletes manage their academics and athletics successfully. If you plan to succeed at both, you will need to utilize these resources and become more diligent and devoted than ever before.

REALITY CHECK:
Your daily level of commitment and discipline often determines your level of success as a student-athlete.

There was a period in my life when I really wanted to become a preacher. I recall going to see my pastor one day in my junior year between my classes and afternoon training. As usual, he listened patiently as I told him how much I wanted to help people. At the end of my little speech, he said something that was so simple yet made a great impact on me. He said I needed to take care of two important things: First, I was still a student who had not yet earned a college degree. Second, I was an athlete who had more feats to accomplish.

He advised me to focus on becoming the best student-athlete that I could be. He was confident that once I committed to doing this properly, everything else would fall into place at the right time. Fortunately, I took his reality check to heart, and it worked well for me. I refocused on excelling as both a student and an athlete by making sure that my academics and athletics were my top daily priorities.

My reality check for you is *always* to remember that you are a student-athlete. The biggest key to doing well as a student-athlete is to be a student first, an athlete second, and everything else afterward. Of course, I am not suggesting that you minimize your religious faith or abandon other personally meaningful activities, but don't forget that your real priorities as a student-athlete are your studies and your athletics.

REALITY CHECK:
You will run into trouble if being a student-athlete is not always your number one priority in college.

I know firsthand that being a student-athlete and not an athlete-student can be challenging at times. For example, you may feel more comfortable playing sports than handling schoolwork. From the start, you may tend to look at yourself as an athlete going to college rather than as a college student competing in sports. You may also know that your athletic ability has given you the opportunity for a college education that your grades or financial situation might not have made possible.

Sometimes, the benefits, special treatment, and higher profile that student-athletes usually receive may also contribute to a sense that you are indeed an athlete-student. Parents, coaches, classmates, and even faculty may reaffirm this misconception by holding you to different standards. At schools where sports are big business, the environment can cater more to athletic performances than to hard work in the classroom. For instance, student-athletes playing certain sports at some schools are unofficially discouraged from choosing tougher majors, like premed, so their studies, classes, and labs don't "interfere" with their athletics. Some professors will automatically give passing grades to certain student-athletes so they can remain eligible. This confusion—being an athlete-student rather than a student-athlete—sets you up for problems throughout your college career.

Even though you will probably spend most of your time around people somehow connected to your school's athletics program, you still are first and foremost a student. As a student-athlete, you also are a member of a relatively small but significant subset of the general student population. Like other students, you have academic responsibilities, including attending and participating in your classes and passing your courses. Unlike them, you also have to spend significant time representing your school in sports. Understanding these similarities and differences gives you a clear perspective on your role at the school.

All student-athletes must meet some standard requirements if they want to play college sports. The NCAA establishes most of these requirements, but your school, its athletic department, coaches, and your conference set many others. Your responsibility is to ensure that you always fulfill all these requirements—academically and otherwise—so you are eligible to compete.

UNDERSTANDING THE ATHLETIC DEPARTMENT

REALITY CHECK:
The athletic department is not a training academy for your sport, nor is it a daycare or automated teller machine (ATM) for student-athletes (even though at some schools it might appear so).

The athletic department is like other departments, such as the social sciences department or business administration department, but it normally has broader functions and a larger staff and budget to help fulfill its role at the school. It usually is responsible for the school's sports-related facilities and equipment, and sometimes even intramural sports.

The main role of the athletic department is to handle most matters concerning students who represent that school in intercollegiate sports—organized sports played against students from other schools. These include complying with the athletic department's governing bodies, such as its respective conference and the NCAA, and offering various resources to develop its student-athletes.

Relatively few schools have financially independent athletic departments. Did you know that most schools usually subsidize their athletics programs? Generally, student-athletes are unaware that most athletic departments lose money, barely break even, or are marginally profitable. Many think that their schools' athletic departments have deeper pockets than they do. I certainly thought that way when I was a freshman.

After our team placed third overall at the NCAA Indoor Championships that spring, some of my teammates and I requested a meeting with our coach in his office to "discuss a few things." Number one on our agenda was to let him know how insulted and embarrassed we were to be one of the best teams in the nation without the latest gear like other top programs. We demanded major upgrades in our shoes and our competition and warm-up clothes. Our coach's face instantly flushed red with disbelief. He was upset because we had ambushed him with accusations of being "old school" and "tight" with money. Eventually he regained his composure and tried to explain his financial decisions, but we thought he was simply making lame excuses.

At the time, I did not appreciate how much the school's struggling football and men's basketball programs indirectly affected our team's budget. Because those teams were not performing very well, our athletic department was not able to generate a lot of revenue. That meant smaller budgets for all sports, including my team. We might have been naïve about how the athletic department *really* worked, but our coach was not foolish. Over the next few weeks, he somehow found a way to keep us all happy by improving our gear. Our "freshly dressed" team finished second overall at the NCAA Outdoor Championships months later.

Your athletic department's budget usually explains many things about your school's athletics program such as which intercollegiate sports are played by your school, how much financial aid is available, the size and quality of the administrative and coaching staff, what equipment or facilities are present, how you travel to competitions, and how much meal money you get on road trips. Being a member school of a major conference or having a nationally ranked team and enjoying a successful postseason in money-earning sports are important to athletic departments because these are key ways that they generate revenue for their entire athletics program.

Bear this in mind the next time you ask your coaches for that extra pair of sneakers—that you really don't need—or to travel by plane instead of busing it. Sometimes, your coaches may not be "cheap" or "tightwads"; they simply may be unable to do certain things because of their team budget.

REALITY CHECK:
Unless you attend a national powerhouse in a major sport, state taxpayers (if you attend a publicly funded school) and your fellow students (often through hidden fees) likely contribute in some financial way to you being there and to whatever benefits you receive as a student-athlete.

COMMON STUDENT-ATHLETE BENEFITS

- Earning a college degree with reduced or no residual financial burdens, such as student loans.
- Improving as a student through free academic resources, such as academic advisors, tutors, and preregistration for classes.
- Developing your athletic abilities through access to better coaching, facilities, equipment, training, and competition gear.

- Competing against the best athletes and teams in your conference, region, and the nation.
- Growing as a person through discipline, hard work, teamwork, commitment, and leadership.
- Expanding your social, personal, and professional networks.
- Traveling and meeting new people.

Regardless of whether you receive some or no direct financial aid from your school, more people invest in your student-athlete experience than you may realize. How you represent your school or make their investments in you pay off depends on you. Despite what some people might think, there is no "free ride." Even when you are on a full scholarship, someone always pays the bill.

YOU CONTROL YOUR FATE

Besides voluntarily quitting the team or your eligibility expiring, how long you play collegiate sports depends on your performance and conduct. Your fate rests in your hands. You are in control of your success.

Your performance in the classroom and on the field, along with your general conduct, makes a difference in your coaches' and administrators' assessments of your value to their programs. We all have heard stories of student-athletes who failed to keep their grades up or who violated important rules because they had the wrong priorities or lost their focus. Staying on top of your schoolwork, training and competing hard, and behaving properly will not only keep you in good standing with professors and coaches but also set the framework for you to do well.

I had a friend who was a decent student and a solid athlete who helped his team to qualify for the NCAA tournament in his sport. Unfortunately, he was also a trouble magnet. Even though he lost his scholarship at one school after getting into trouble, his behavior did not change after getting another chance at a different school. Eventually, he was kicked off his new team after police arrested him for selling drugs. He wasted all his talent and hard work because of his poor choices away from the field, and others paid a heavy price for his actions. Although he did not intend to harm his team, his absence from the squad and the chaos surrounding his arrest negatively affected his teammates, who struggled for the rest of the season. Because he lacked the maturity and self-discipline to do the right things, his bright college career came to a premature end.

No matter what school you attend, what sport you play, or what role you play on your team, always remember that you are a representative of your school and there are certain rules that you must follow. All your choices on and off the field must be consistent with being a student-athlete regardless of where you go, including on campus, at parties, and even on road trips. Some student-athletes mistakenly think that they can act however they want during their off-seasons, holidays, or spring breaks. They forget, underestimate, or ignore how their actions can jeopardize their eligibility, financial aid, roles on their squads, or status at their schools. Although you are young, you still are responsible for your choices, actions, and behavior at all times. Remember, the rules governing student-athletes don't temporarily stop or change just because you may want them to.

REALITY CHECK:
Being a student-athlete affects you
twenty-four hours a day, 365 days a year.

All coaches, administrators, faculty, and staff prefer working with student-athletes who add value to their programs or classes, who won't create distractions, and who aren't high maintenance. Many talented student-athletes handicap their progress or become liabilities because they don't develop or practice the qualities needed to succeed in college. On the other hand, thousands of less athletically gifted student-athletes achieve more than they and others initially believed possible. They add value to their teams because they possess the right attitudes to be winners in college.

Your success as a student-athlete relies on your personal profile—positive or negative. I have seen walk-ons with positive personal profiles replace scholarship athletes with negative personal profiles as starters or key players on their teams because they proved more reliable, committed, and hard working—traits most coaches value. Fortunately, you can learn many of these winning traits, several of which will be discussed throughout this book.

TRAITS OF SUCCESSFUL AND UNSUCCESSFUL STUDENT-ATHLETES

Positive Personal Profile

- *Self-motivation*—Does not need babysitters
- *Self-discipline*—Has self-control and is willing to sacrifice now for something better later
- *Industriousness*—Gives consistently high levels of effort on and off the field
- *High personal integrity*—Does not take illegal shortcuts to reach goals and is trustworthy
- *Dependability*—Can be counted on without constant nudging

- *Respect*—Has high regard for self, others, and authority
- *Accountability*—Honors responsibilities to others
- *Punctuality*—Is present, and starts and finishes, on time
- *Organization*—Creates goals and makes plans to reach them
- *Self-confidence*—Believes in his ability to excel

Negative Personal Profile

- *Low personal drive*—Must be prodded to do what needs to be done
- *Lack of self-discipline*—Does not like to sacrifice short-term gratification for later gains
- *Poor work ethic*—Prefers taking the easy road
- *Low personal integrity*—Reaches goals through any method, even illegally; untrustworthy
- *Undependability*—Cannot be counted on
- *Trouble with authority*—Tends to question or undermine authority or is trouble prone
- *Low personal accountability*—Disrespects the need to be answerable to others
- *Poor time management*—Is always rushing, late, or procrastinating
- *Acceptance of mediocrity and failure*—Sets sights too low, is not bothered by being average, or becomes defined by setbacks
- *Low self-esteem*—Is unsure of his identity, his role, or his purpose

BALANCING ACT: STUDENT + ATHLETE = STUDENT-ATHLETE

During and after college, many people helped me to "keep it real" along the way. In this book, I want to pass on to you some of this advice and encouragement. Because you wear two hats as a student and as an athlete, you probably have to juggle more balls at the same time than regular students do. However, you also have access to many more benefits and opportunities than they do at minimal or no cost to you.

You control your fate as a student-athlete through your performance in the classroom and on the field, and by your general conduct. Wherever you go, always proudly represent your team and your school. All your choices on and off the field should be consistent with being a student-athlete.

Your continued success as a student-athlete depends on your commitment to develop your positive profile and to maintain the proper balance between *student* and *athlete*. Remember, when you start strong with the fundamentals of being a student-athlete, you greatly increase your chances of success in all areas of your college life.

ONE-ON-ONE

- **What are you doing to avoid being an athlete-student rather than a student-athlete?**

- **How does your athletic department's budget affect you?**

- **What are some of the benefits of being a student-athlete?**

- **How are you now controlling your success?**

- **What traits do you need to change about yourself to be more successful as a collegiate student-athlete?**

②

SET NEW PERSONAL BESTS

Imagine setting out to sea all alone on a boat with no compass, no map, or no destination. Let's take it a step further. What would happen if you also didn't have oars to help you steer when you hit rough waves or an anchor to stop when you wanted to? You'd probably never do this because you know how disastrous being at the mercy of the sea could be, yet this is exactly the type of thing that happens to many student-athletes. They leave home; go to college; forget where they came from, how they got there, and what they should be doing; and find themselves just drifting without a real purpose or plan for their lives.

REALITY CHECK:
Because you have only a relatively short time as a student-athlete, you can't afford to drift too far or for too long.

Your biggest challenge as a young person may be dealing with what I call the "drift effect." In college, you will encounter new people, ideas, and situations, many of which will act like sea waves or storms in your life. They will constantly push and pull you in many directions—some good, some bad. If you are not anchored or if you feel unsure about who you are, what you believe, and where you want to go, then you probably will eventually give in to the waves, drift, and fail to be as successful as you could be. In fact, if you are not careful, you may get caught up in situations that can cause you to miss once-in-a-lifetime opportunities or even find yourself in trouble.

Throughout college, I had countless experiences that tested my judgment and character. New situations and new value systems frequently challenged me, especially during my first two years. Even with self-confidence and a strong religious upbringing, I still felt peer pressure, and I was not always strong enough to resist. Many times I found myself drifting along, making choices that I felt ashamed about later on. This usually happened when I followed others without thinking about doing what was right or best for me.

For example, when I was a freshman, some of my teammates would sneak into a coach's office after he left for the day to make international phone calls. Although I knew it was wrong, I still followed them. I justified it by telling myself that "everyone was doing it" and that I was "saving my parents money"—if they had only known. One Friday, after that coach had left, we raided his unlocked office to tag-team the phone. Because I was the freshman, they left me outside to be the watchman just in case he returned unexpectedly.

When it was my turn to use the phone, I asked if someone would look out for me and was assured that I had nothing to worry about because we were a "team." Right! Three minutes into my call to a friend, I heard the doorknob suddenly creak.

I immediately hung up, knowing that something was wrong although no one had given me the secret "cough" or knock on the door warning me to escape. I turned around and found the coach staring at me curiously. I was busted! I quickly made up a lame excuse about looking for printer paper and darted past him before he could think twice about my flimsy reason for being in his office, alone on a Friday afternoon, without his permission.

My teammates looked surprised to see me arrive at the weight room so soon, drenched in sweat. When I asked who was looking out for me, they all busted out laughing. Then I got it—the joke was on me! How stupid could I be? There I was risking trouble by following guys I had known for only a few weeks, when I knew better and had no backup—a classic freshman mistake.

I should have figured out that something like that would have happened to me. A few weeks earlier, on the Friday before the start of my first college semester, two of those same teammates had asked me if I wanted to "roll" with them to "check out the town." Although I had just met them for the first time earlier that day, I gladly agreed because I was tired of being cooped up in my dorm room for freshman orientation. I hopped into the car without thinking twice about whether I should trust them because, after all, we were "teammates." Of course, none of my new "teammates" told me that our real destination was a rundown porn shop on the outskirts of town before we left. I was pretty upset when I realized that we had not accidentally parked in front of the store with the flickering "XXX" neon sign. At first I stood my ground and stayed in the car, determined not to "compromise" my religious beliefs. However, after some of the not-too-friendly-looking clientele outside the shop started looking in my direction for a split-second too long, I decided to "take one for the team" and soon joined them inside. Even though most of my teammates were good people who did the right thing, sometimes I allowed myself to get caught up in circumstances that I knew were wrong or not the best ones for me.

Apart from my own experiences, I saw how drifting negatively affected the lives of some teammates and other student-athletes. I remember the case of a freshman student-athlete from a small town who was rooming with an older student-athlete from a vastly different background. Unfortunately, their coach did not realize that the older roommate, a new transfer to the school, was not exactly a good role model. Within weeks after the start of their first semester, the freshman had lost sight of why he was in college. Instead of being a good mentor, his roommate introduced him to the world of getting drunk, getting high, and getting into trouble. The situation worsened in the next semester. Struggling with his grades, athletics, and personal issues, he quit school in the middle of the season and never returned. His college career ended as a freshman.

I learned that you eventually drift—lose touch with your identity and your direction—if you don't stay true to yourself on a regular basis.

BE TRUE TO YOURSELF

"This above all: to thine own self be true . . ." *Hamlet*, William Shakespeare

When I was younger, my father often used this famous quote as one of his favorite reality checks to get me to think carefully about my choices—whether a specific action served me well at that time. Was I doing my best? Was my choice consistent with my core values and goals? Of course, the assumption at the heart of this challenge was that I already knew my "own self." To be honest, sometimes I had pretty good insight into my life; other times I was not as sure about who I was.

REALITY CHECK:
You can't consistently stay true to yourself if you don't really know or understand your core identity.

UNDERSTANDING YOUR PERSONAL VALUES AND CORE IDENTITY

Regardless of your talents and ambitions, your core identity influences your success and affects the overall quality of your life. Who you are at the core is made up of your thoughts, feelings, and attitudes. They influence many things about your life, including how you use your abilities and how you handle various circumstances and opportunities. Your core identity usually reflects your personal value system. Your personal values affect your choices. The sum of those choices determines who and where you are in life, and this cycle continues for the rest of your life.

Your personal value system is the consistent set of personal ethics that govern your life. In other words, it is what you believe is right and wrong. Your value system starts to form during your childhood and continues to develop throughout your life. Your individual nature, environment, experiences, choices, and upbringing all shape it.

Your relationships with those closest to you, such as your family, friends, significant others, and coaches, usually play the biggest role in shaping your value system. Their influences will often continue to affect your choices even when they are not present. Sometimes, people you've never met but find inspiring, such as role models or personal heroes, may also help to influence your values. Besides my family's influence, many of my personal values were shaped by my good friends, coaches, personal experiences, and my religious background.

Here's a good exercise. Put down the book and take a minute to think about and write down who or what has most influenced your value system and in what ways. (Come on now, that wasn't a minute!) The results may surprise you and may probably explain a lot about why you are who you are. My list certainly did.

Your personal value system acts as your personal GPS unit. It either guides you toward or away from your purpose or what you should be doing. You will feel greater personal fulfillment the closer you are to your purpose. The further away you move from your values, the more likely you are to seek true satisfaction in potentially destructive relationships, circumstances, and behaviors. Even celebrities fall victim to drug and alcohol abuse or destructive lifestyles because their core identities are out of whack or they live without a greater sense of purpose.

REALITY CHECK:
If who you are on the inside is not properly grounded and heading in the right direction, then you become more likely to get into trouble and stray from the best path for your life.

PERFORMANCE DOES NOT EQUAL IDENTITY

Be careful not to define yourself mainly by your performances as a student or as an athlete. You are not the sum of your accomplishments. For example, imagine a trouble-prone teammate with a poor work ethic and a terrible attitude toward others. Despite these character flaws, she plays well because of her great athleticism. Now imagine another teammate who is respectful, hard working, and trustworthy. Unfortunately, her game is average because she lacks great natural athletic abilities. In both cases, how this teammate performs as an athlete does not truly reflect who she is as a person. However great your performances, they do not add up to who you are.

Early in my career, I used to base how I felt about myself and my life on how I performed at competitions. When I did well, everything was great. When I performed poorly or below my expectations, the whole world seemed like a dark and cold place—until I competed well again. Looking back, I am sure that I would have trained and performed consistently better without those negative emotions and thoughts burdening me, and sometimes those who had to deal with me, between my better competition results.

Although who you are and how you perform tend to be interrelated, knowing the difference can help you to put your results in their proper perspective. I know that as an athlete, this can be challenging because of all the hard work you put in and the pressures from yourself and others to perform well. However, because everyone has different abilities and opportunities, no two people will perform in the same way or with the same results. Your performances will vary—one day they may be terrific, and another day they may suck. So step off the dangerous and illogical emotional roller coaster of judging yourself and others based mainly on performances.

WHO IS THE *REAL* YOU?

Knowing oneself is not an easy task. While most of us are self-aware and know our own stories, few of us take the time to analyze ourselves. Self-analysis helps us to discover why we think, say, and do certain things, but it also requires taking time for some serious personal reflection. Many people live their entire lives without figuring out their core identity, and so they continue to make choices that prevent them from reaching their full potential or achieving a lasting sense of fulfillment.

Sadly, countless student-athletes don't figure out that who they are and where they are heading directly impact how successful they become. Far too many former student-athletes look back at their college careers with lifelong regrets about not doing more during those pivotal years of their lives because they did not look at themselves more closely. Fortunately, you don't have to follow in their footsteps. The tips and reality checks in this book will help you to take a deeper look at yourself so you can make the most of your college days.

Once you start developing a clear and accurate picture of your "own self," you will be ahead of many others your age—in fact, well ahead of many people older than you too. You will also be on your way to making choices that guide you to the successes you should have and avoiding the many pitfalls awaiting those who don't really know or stay true to themselves.

Let's now take a look at three methods you can use to discover more about the *real* you.

Look into your mirror—There is no such thing as an objective self-assessment. Even when answering questions on a personal evaluation form, you still give your opinion of yourself. Your answers may not be scientifically verifiable, or they may not correspond with reality.

REALITY CHECK:
If you want a more accurate picture
of who you really are, you will need to take
longer, harder, and more frequent looks at
yourself in the mirror.

The reality of looking at ourselves in the mirror is one of the hardest and scariest things we can do. Whenever we look into the mirror for too long or too closely, we eventually see things that we don't like about ourselves. Some people ignore what they dislike about themselves and focus only on their "good side." Others become so preoccupied with their imperfections that they stop looking at themselves altogether. Many people in our culture put a premium on entertainment, such as movies, sports, and music, because it transports them to "another world" full of the exceptional or the impossible. They often use such diversions from reality to escape looking into their own mirrors or analyzing their lives in a deep way. As a result, they fail to address their personal issues properly or make improvements in their lives that could lead them to greater success and personal fulfillment.

Highly successful people, in contrast, generally don't fear taking frequent looks at themselves, especially in areas where they excel. Unlike the evil stepmother in the fairy tale *Snow White*, when they say, "Mirror, mirror on the wall," they really want to see a true reflection of themselves—the good and the bad. They don't run away from this reflection, even when it is tough to swallow. Successful people know how to improve themselves and reach their goals by effectively using their personal mirrors to identify what they need to improve and to bring focus to their lives.

Looking at a physical mirror gives you instant feedback, but looking at your inner mirror is far more abstract and challenging. You must often ask yourself probing questions to get a true reflection of who you are at the core. Doing a deep self-assessment can be intimidating and a lot to handle, especially as a young adult. Many people don't ask themselves important questions about why they make certain choices or behave in particular ways because they are unsure of how to do it, afraid of what they might discover, or just don't think it is important. However, if you don't take the time to look at yourself regularly and closely, then how can you consistently make the best choices for your life? Answer: You consistently can't! That's like your coach giving you workouts throughout the season without watching you train and expecting you to just go out and win a championship.

In practical terms, looking at yourself in the mirror is like visiting the doctor when you feel ill. Even if your symptoms are mostly external, besides doing a physical examination, the doctor will likely ask you a series of questions ranging from when your symptoms started to your family medical history. Sometimes these questions may seem unrelated to your symptoms, but the answers to those questions help the doctor make a more accurate diagnosis of your condition, which is necessary for prescribing the correct treatment.

Similarly, you need to learn to ask yourself a wide range of questions as a doctor does to a patient or a lawyer does to a client or witness. This question-and-answer process can really help you to step outside of yourself and become more "objective" so that you can see yourself better. This includes learning more about your strengths, weaknesses, preferences, tendencies, and fears, as well as what makes you tick— important information when considering the best choices for you in different circumstances.

Remember, making an honest effort to improve in any area always starts with taking an honest look at yourself in the mirror.

Listen to your inner voice—How often have you said to yourself, "Something told me to . . ." or "I knew I should have. . ."? If you are like me, then too many times to count. I believe that we all have an "inner voice" whose role is to give us guidance about our purpose in life. I'm not talking about something that is spooky or strange; I'm talking about something most people call "conscience."

Make a regular effort to find and listen to your inner voice because it will usually lead you down the best path for your life. Ignoring or not listening carefully to it will often cause you to make poor or regrettable decisions. For example, you're more likely to become a follower and not a leader because you end up being tied to the opinions and choices of others instead of being strong in your personal resolve to do what is best for you.

Learning to listen to your own inner voice can be challenging, especially in this hyperstimulating, fast-paced world. It often means purposely taking time away from common daily distractions like TV, the Internet, telephones, and the ever-present opportunity to socialize or party. Although some people use this time to pray or meditate, you may choose to do whatever you find satisfying or meaningful to you.

Let others help you—To help you round out your personal assessment, consider the input of others, such as your family, friends, teammates, and professors. They may be able to give you solid evaluations and advice because they often see traits in you that you cannot detect on your own. Although you may feel a natural temptation to accept their observations or opinions as your main source of information about yourself, don't. What they say should help you complete your assessment, not become the main gauge or compass for your life. In other words, don't take everything people say about you wholesale, without question.

Take some time to filter and reflect on their comments and opinions. Use their input for additional guidance, not as a substitute for doing your own background work, especially when making important choices in areas such as your academics, athletics, and social life. Keep in mind that some comments may appear negative at first but may prove valid later. Don't get bent out of shape about constructive criticism, especially when it seems too personal. Think of it as advice to improve your "performance in living" so you can become the best you can be. Extract what is true, relevant, and useful, and apply the good advice to your life.

REALITY CHECK:
You can't fulfill your purpose if you always follow the opinions, comments, or actions of others, regardless of who they are.

MIRROR, MIRROR ON THE WALL

I constantly had "conversations" with myself about what I was doing and where my life was heading. Sometimes, I just stared at myself in my dorm room mirror and asked myself tough questions about my attitudes, my motives, and my character. For instance, was I doing something with a hidden agenda? Was I acting out of fear, or anger, or love? Was I being fair or compassionate toward others? Was I running away from something that I should be addressing more directly? Did my conversations and actions reflect my personal values and core beliefs? Did I do something out of personal conviction or simply because it was easy to do or so that I could fit in? Some days, I wrote down these questions and answers.

It always amazed me how dishonest with myself I could become when the questions got too personal. Although I already knew most of the answers, sometimes I tried not to acknowledge them and therefore not have to deal with them. It wasn't always easy to look at things I did not like about myself and things I needed to improve. For instance, I saw insecurities about myself that I tried to cover up and "skeletons" that I didn't want others to discover. I found contradictions between some of my words and actions, as well as many things that I did not understand about myself. However, I also saw several good things about myself, which encouraged me to keep going, especially when I felt down or when I was uncertain about my abilities or the right decision to make.

Besides questioning myself, I tried to listen to my inner voice whenever I had to make important choices. This often meant taking a break from my hectic routine and the chorus of other peoples' voices all around me during the day. Usually the best time for me to do this was right before I went to sleep at night because it was quiet and I did not have to worry about interruptions. Most times my inner voice guided me away from trouble, toward what was best for me in the long term. Sometimes I missed it or purposely ignored it, particularly when I was determined to do something regardless of the consequences. Of course, in some way, it also gave me the old "I told you so" after I foolishly disregarded it and situations turned out worse than they should have.

I also learned to trust those closest to me to look for blind spots in my character and flaws in my thinking. They knew me best and could usually sense when my values and views were off base or when I was just not acting right. Even though I did not always like what they told me or follow their suggestions, I usually gave their opinions some thought when assessing myself and before I acted.

KEEP UP YOUR CORE TRAINING

As in athletics, your core strength provides stability for whatever you do. A strong core often supports your success; a weak core undermines you. It is important that your core values be strong and positive from the very start. Some student-athletes, for example, think that cheating on an exam, plagiarizing a paper, lying when they are in a jam, acting in an unsportsmanlike way, or being involved in illegal activities are okay. They are not!

REALITY CHECK:
A personal value system that encourages breaking rules or living on the edge of trouble may give you some good results or be exciting now, but it usually turns out to be counterproductive and costly later on.

You can do well but not have lasting success or personal satisfaction in college and beyond because of warped and unethical values. Eventually, like geographical fault lines, personal character flaws and other core issues that you don't correct or address properly can erupt under certain circumstances and damage your opportunities, reputation, relationships, quality of life, and well-being. However, you can do well and fully enjoy your achievements by living with integrity, discipline, personal responsibility, a positive attitude, and a strong work ethic.

Constantly evaluate and reevaluate what is motivating and influencing you and your choices. In the process, you will likely need to change some of your personal values or add new ones. For example, you may need to cut some negative relationships or develop healthier ones. You may have to change your environment and monitor the books, music, movies, and conversations that constantly feed your mind so you can be more positive. I know from experience that these changes can be difficult, especially when ending certain relationships or dropping old habits, but they are doable. Being honest with yourself and regularly cleaning your mirror of negativity and gunk can have a significant, positive impact on how you view yourself and live your daily life—important keys to success.

CREATE YOUR PERSONAL MISSION STATEMENT

Writing a personal mission statement about your core identity and your plan in life is one of the best ways to tie everything together and bring focus to your life. Your personal mission statement should capture the essence of *you*. Creating one may seem like an intimidating task, but it really isn't. Here are a few useful tips to get you started:

Characteristics of a Strong Personal Mission Statement

- *Meaningful*—Make it relevant and truthful to your life.
- *Reflecting your personal values*—Include things consistent with your character, values, and motivation.
- *Personal*—Keep the focus on you, not on impressing others.
- *Clear*—Be specific about what actions, behaviors, goals, and attitudes you want to display or achieve.
- *Simple*—You don't need fancy words or phrases.
- *Brief*—Keep it between three and five lines long.
- *Positive*—Focus on what will encourage and inspire you to do better.

- *Flexible*—Expect changes as you grow and learn as a person and an athlete. It's okay to adjust your personal statement when necessary.

Here's an example of a mission statement I created:

To use my abilities, faith, knowledge, and resources to become a better person, student, and athlete while helping others to improve their lives however I can. I understand that the only way to fulfill my mission is through willingness to learn, resilience in the face of challenges, and a proactive attitude.

REALITY CHECK:
Without some kind of personal mission statement, your life will lack proper focus and direction.

Spend a few moments creating one and remember that it doesn't need to be "perfect"—no one is grading it. Write it down so you can remember it and refer to it later. Also try to keep it somewhere easily accessible and visible, such as in your wallet or posted prominently in your room. This way, it can be a daily guide and a source of encouragement for you. You may also consider regularly reading it aloud to yourself or giving a copy of it to someone, such as your best friend or a teammate, who can hold you accountable to it.

WHAT TYPE OF STUDENT AND ATHLETE ARE YOU?

Besides figuring out who you are as a person, it is important that you also assess yourself as a student-athlete. Being clear about your strengths and weaknesses as a student and as an athlete will give you a better idea of where you stand, how you got there, and where you are heading. This information can help you decide how best to use your time and resources to improve in those areas. You probably already have some idea of your abilities as a student and as an athlete from prior testing and performances, so start your self-assessment with these results. For example, when assessing yourself as a student, look at your transcripts and grades. As an athlete, start with your career averages and personal records. Be careful not to rely on "outliers," which are performances or outcomes significantly different—positive or negative—from your normal results. These marks show your potential range of results, not your average performances on regular days.

REALITY CHECK:
Your average performances are the
real measures of where you are now, not
your all-time best results.

I slashed my personal best in the 100-meter dash early in the season of my freshman year. While I was cooling down, my coach approached me with one of his past athletes, a former NCAA 100-meter dash champion. After their congratulations, they warned me not to get a "big head" because although I had just run one of the fastest times in the world for that year, I was not yet at "that level." Outwardly, I nodded in agreement, but inwardly I was insulted. Why were they trying to kill my "buzz" only minutes after my best performance? What did they know? I had "arrived," or so I thought. How right they were. My performances for the rest of that season were only slightly better than my previous personal best. In fact, not until my junior year, after much hard work and steady progress, did I finally lower my personal best in that event and my average race times become closer to that outlier from my freshman season. I learned that what I could reliably do on most days was a better indicator of how good an athlete I was at that time than my all-time best mark.

After making a basic review of your performance history, think about the factors that might have affected your normal results. Here are some questions that you can ask yourself:

As a student, did you make your studies a priority? Did you take good notes and pay attention in class? Did you take enough time to prepare for exams and write papers? Did you have instructors who were knowledgeable and made the classes interesting? Do you have natural weaknesses or strengths in some subject areas?

As an athlete, how serious were you about competing? Did you have good coaches, a solid training system, and good team chemistry? Did you have the proper training facilities and equipment? How tough were your opponents and competition schedule? Did you have a proper precompetition warm-up routine? Were you injured?

Make a written note of how certain factors may have affected your usual results and even your outliers. Carefully examine these factors and look for trends in, for instance, your attitudes, habits, preparations, game plan, execution, or how you responded to certain people or circumstances. Putting your results in their right perspective helps you identify areas that usually help or hurt your performances—an important step toward improving in each of these areas and as a student-athlete.

NOT EXACTLY MR. PERFECT

I usually tried to practice what I "preached"—well, at least some form of it. In reality, like most other young people, I often struggled with staying true to my identity and to my values. Quite frankly, sometimes it was easier to try to fit in by following others even though I knew the path was not right or the best one for me. Many times I lost my way and sense of purpose because I was stubborn, lazy, or too scared to look into my mirror or follow my inner voice.

Overall, I think that the solid support system of family and friends, my personal faith, and really trying to stay true to my values helped me not to drift too far or for too long. Let me stress again that this was not always easy, and I did some things in college I am ashamed of, but I eventually cleaned up my act (most times).

BE PATIENT WITH YOURSELF

Finally, understanding and accepting yourself can take you on quite a journey. Be open-minded and patient with yourself. Your collegiate experience represents a significant part of this journey, so do your best to avoid the many potholes in the road, such as the "drift effect." This is a unique time in your life to evaluate yourself and grow as a student, as an athlete, and as a person. Creating a personal mission statement will help you to become more focused as you tie everything together in a few meaningful words. Making positive changes to your value system can be challenging, especially if your environment has been filled with negativity or you come from an unsupportive background. Remember, countless people have positively transformed their lives and you can too.

Be consistent, honest, and patient with yourself so that you can come out on the other side of your college experience as a well-rounded and better student, athlete, and person. Keep looking in the mirror and listening to your inner voice, and you will set new personal bests.

ONE-ON-ONE

- What is the "drift effect" and in what way has it affected your life?

- Name three methods you can use to understand your core identity.

- How are positive or negative values driving your daily choices?

- What is your personal mission statement? How does it influence you?

- What are some of your strengths and weaknesses as a student and as an athlete? How do they help or hurt you as a student-athlete?

MASTER THE PLAYBOOK

Imagine life without rules. Cool, right? Think about that again. Imagine playing sports, driving, or doing business without rules or directions. Not only would there be chaos, but you could also be the victim of your choices or those of others. For instance, consider how many more accidents would happen without traffic lights, speed limits, or laws about driving under the influence (DUI). Rules provide guidelines, direction, and protection. Knowing and following rules always makes you more successful. A stomach-wrenching experience taught me this lesson.

Although I knew it was against the rules to use hotplates in my college's dorms, I bought one anyway. Like many other students living in the dorms, I planned to save money by using it to cook my own dinners. Because I did not know how to cook before I came to college, during my first semester I had been limited to eating Uncle Ben's microwaveable rice and canned tuna fish every day. During my second semester, the hotplate allowed me to graduate to cooking meatless pasta dishes, which gave me false confidence in my "underground" cooking skills.

One day after practice, I went down the hall to visit a teammate who was using his hotplate to cook dinner. Truth be told, I was hoping to sneak a meal from him because I was hungry and too lazy to cook. After sampling his Hamburger Helper, I was inspired to upgrade my menu. I assumed that if he could do it, then I could too, so I asked him what I needed to buy.

The next day, I returned from the grocery store psyched about making my first Hamburger Helper meal. Rather than reading the directions on the box, I just dumped everything, including the raw ground beef, into the pan. Just as I had done with my packaged pasta, I covered the pan and let the mixture simmer while I watched TV. Ten minutes later, I sat down to eat my latest culinary masterpiece. Perhaps I should have known that something was not right. The food looked, smelled, and tasted different from what I had eaten the night before. Like many people on a tight budget, I kept shoveling it down even though it was barely edible because I had prepared it and did not want to waste money.

Later in the evening, I began developing severe stomach cramps, so I called my "Hamburger Helper" teammate down the hall. He asked how long I had cooked the meat *before* I put in the rest of the ingredients.

"How long did I do what?"

He started laughing and told me that I probably had food poisoning from not cooking the ground beef properly. He was right. For the next few days, I was sick in bed.

Of course, the moral of the story boils down to two lessons: I broke one rule that I knew—hotplates were forbidden in the dorms—and one that I had not bothered to learn—frozen meat needs thorough cooking before eating.

Most student-athletes prefer to jump into the college experience headfirst and learn the rules later. The majority of them complete college without major problems, but not everyone ends up so lucky. Many pay a heavy price for not knowing or following the rules, like me when I tried to cook Hamburger Helper. Hopefully, this book can help make you one of the smarter and luckier ones who use the rules to your benefit.

During freshman orientation, most schools give out handbooks that outline important guidelines and policies all student-athletes should know and follow. Few take the time to read their handbooks carefully, and most only flip through a few pages before setting them aside. I know that reading through those books can be boring, but here's something to think about: When you learn and follow the rules from the start, you can avoid unnecessary problems and drama later.

IGNORANCE IS NOT BLISS

REALITY CHECK:
Contrary to the popular saying, ignorance is *not* bliss, especially when dealing with the NCAA—what you don't know *can* hurt you.

Every year, the NCAA amends and adds regulations to its voluminous rulebook, which governs all manner of NCAA-related matters. Collegiate coaches, compliance officers, and some athletic administrators must take annual NCAA certification exams to ensure that they stay on top of the latest rules. For them, ignorance of the rules is not an option.

NCAA violators could endanger their jobs and put their schools at risk of sanctions, such as forfeiting scholarships, games or championships, or being denied a chance at postseason play. NCAA violations can potentially ruin a school's reputation, in turn jeopardizing recruiting, competition attendance, and sponsorships. At some schools, such sanctions could mean the loss of millions of dollars and years before a successful and profitable program is rebuilt. This means athletic administrators and coaches must know the rules and comply with them. The same applies to you as a student-athlete. The consequences of ignorance could be very costly.

RULES, RULES, RULES

Who likes to hear the word "rules" except those who make them? Generally, that word relates to restrictions, and most of us do not like feeling restricted. At every stage of your collegiate career, some rules—actually many rules—will govern your life. Because your school wants to avoid NCAA sanctions caused by student-athlete violations, you will have to obey a stricter set of rules than regular students follow. However, remember that as a student-athlete, you likely have greater opportunities and privileges than they do.

Since rules play a big part in your collegiate life, it's best just to accept them. Find out now what they are and what they mean so you can comply with them on a daily basis. Remember, the rules are made for you to follow.

REALITY CHECK:
If you lack the interest or discipline to follow the rules governing you as a student-athlete, you will eventually end up in trouble.

Organizations and individuals whose rules you will have to follow include:

- NCAA
- Sport-specific (basketball, baseball, rowing, lacrosse, etc.) governing body
- Conference
- Athletic department
- Team
- School
- Professors

HOW TO LEARN THE RULES

Here are three simple ways to learn the rules and any other information you need to know in college: reading, observing, and asking questions.

Read the rules. Most college-related rules can be found in handbooks or guides, which colleges make available in printed form or online. For example, you will probably find your athletic department's rules printed in a student-athlete handbook, while your school's rules, which apply to all enrolled students, are likely published online as well as in print. Your coaches may have written team rules, but most will tend to come from what they say or imply.

The NCAA posts its rules online, as do most conferences and athletic organizations. Professors usually explain the rules for their courses in their syllabuses, which they hand out for you to read at the start of the semester. You can also request most of these materials in writing from the appropriate person, department, or organization in case you misplaced or never received them.

Observation, using your eyes and ears, is another good way to learn the rules. Although generally not as reliable as reading, observation is a useful way to learn many "unofficial" rules. Get in the habit of observing your environment and figuring out how things *really* work. Observation can also help you to understand unspoken team-related issues. For instance, to avoid trouble from the NCAA or your conference, your coach might not explicitly state certain team rules or policies, yet you are expected to figure out and follow these unspoken and unwritten "rules." This often applies to off-season training.

Because the NCAA restricts coaches in some sports from giving athletes formal workouts during certain periods, coaches often get around these rules by making workout "suggestions," which you are expected to follow. You must figure out that, although your coach cannot force you to practice because of the official rules, not following their "suggestions" *will* result in negative consequences for you later.

Unspoken rules also apply to team dynamics. Take time to observe and learn about your teammates and coaches. These observations can be very helpful in developing your role on the team and your relationships with others, especially your coaches. For example, through observation you can figure out the "pecking order" on your team, which teammates to trust, or what you need to do to get more playing time from your coach.

During my first years in college, I found some unofficial rules harder to accept than others. For example, in the beginning, I could not understand why basketball and football players always got preferential treatment in the training room and athletic department and more exposure in the media and the local community. I felt peeved, especially because my track team was nationally ranked in the top five while theirs struggled to have good seasons. No official handbook explained why revenue-generating sports usually got different or better benefits compared to most Olympic or women's sports. However, I soon learned the unofficial "rule" that not all sports and performances were equal for a reason—money talks!

In general, basketball and football teams put more "butts in seats" and pull in more dollars at the concession stands than other sports. Those players always enjoyed the best the school had to offer its student-athletes, even when their teams were not the best ones on campus. I experienced this firsthand one year after losing the Male Student-Athlete of the Year Award at my school to a higher profile athlete in a revenue-generating sport. Even he seemed shocked at winning the award because I was heavily favored due to my outstanding results in the conference and nationally. This was a tough pill to swallow—my coach was pretty upset about it too—but I eventually accepted the economic and political reality of "the game." As I said, money talks!

Even professors and teaching assistants have personal rules and preferences that you won't find in their syllabuses. Through observation, you might pick up some useful information about what they expect or won't tolerate from students, knowledge that could help you to improve your grades or reputation in their classes.

Although observation can be a powerful way to learn, it can also cause problems because of misinterpretation. Observation usually does not provide a good defense if you violate a rule, especially when your actions go against a written rule. For example, justifying your choices by saying that "everyone does it" does not make you less responsible for your actions or automatically get you off the hook, even if most others do break or bend that written rule. Written rules leave less room for misinterpretation. You should use observation to make yourself aware of unofficial rules or practices but not as a replacement for written rules.

Asking a question can often be the simplest and most direct way of learning. Don't let shyness, laziness, stubbornness, arrogance, or shame keep you silent. If you feel unsure about anything, always locate and ask the right source to learn what the rules say. Don't make the mistake of relying on those who don't have the correct qualifications or authorization to answer, especially for important matters. Following the wrong answers could have serious consequences. Although other people may provide you with useful information, consider this information as "unofficial" until confirmed by the right person or by the latest official written rules. Don't base important decisions on assumptions or hearsay, however well-intended the advice may be.

Depending on the question, you might ask your parents, friends, coaches, members of the staff, or even teammates for direction. For instance, for critical issues, such as dealing with boosters, accepting gifts, transferring, or redshirting, you should ask your compliance officer for guidance. For academic matters, you may talk with your academic advisors, professors, or teaching assistants. For athletic issues, a coach, trainer, or teammate can probably answer your questions. As a rule, the more important the question, the more important it is for you to go to the right source for the correct answer from the start. Again, whenever a discrepancy occurs between what is said and what is written, always rely on the latest official written rules for your protection.

Although I used my syllabuses and a few other important documents for guidance, I mostly observed and asked questions. I thought that I could reach my goals more easily by learning how best to operate within the different systems at the school. So I usually stepped back and observed people carefully to figure out how things really worked in the classroom, on my team, and in whatever circumstances I faced. I always tried to ask questions when I felt unsure or wanted to confirm that I was correct before I acted. Pretending I knew all the answers didn't benefit me and could cause me trouble later on. I also spoke with anyone, including professors, advisors, teammates, and even janitorial staff, who had been at the school for some time.

I pieced together information from them and added what I learned on my own, and it worked well for me. I recommend taking your time to learn about the rules and the "players" in a system first rather than blindly jumping into circumstances or relationships. This not only helps you to figure out what is really going on, who people really are, and what roles they play, but also where you best fit in.

As my parents were so far away, they constantly reminded me that I needed to avoid as much trouble as I could because they were not right around the corner to help me, plus they had invested so much in me. I also saw firsthand how breaking or bending rules—innocently or not—hurt teammates, other student-athletes, and the school. I did not want that kind of college experience. Although I was not Mr. Goody Two-Shoes, I tried not to let anyone or anything ruin my plans for success in college. Knowing and staying within the rules played a big part in achieving that success.

Besides learning the rules to avoid trouble, I also wanted to know them so that I could take advantage of any legitimate opportunity to become better. Sometimes we get so caught up with what the rules forbid us to do that we overlook how they can empower us to succeed. Contrary to how it may seem, most rules governing student-athletes are designed to help you avoid situations that can negatively influence your success. For example, it is illegal for student-athletes to bet on sports. By restricting your ability to gamble, these rules increase your chances of succeeding as a student-athlete because you (a) practice the important life skills of fair play and hard work and (b) avoid becoming involved with people or in circumstances that could land you in trouble legally, financially, and otherwise.

Instead of always looking at the rules governing your time as a student-athlete as restricting your actions, perhaps you should consider them as guidelines for success. This approach will allow you to see more opportunities and advantages that following them gives you.

KNOW YOUR RIGHTS

Learning the rules informs you not only about what you should do but also about what to expect of others. Take time to learn about your rights because ignorance of them might leave you open to victimization from others. For example, some coaches still threaten to cut athletes' financial aid based solely on athletic performances. While this practice commonly occurred in the past, the NCAA now forbids it. Still, many student-athletes suffer unnecessarily because they are unaware of their rights on this issue. Similarly, you should learn your rights about sexual harassment, discrimination, abuse, improper conduct, and many other important issues related to your college experiences on and off campus.

REALITY CHECK:
Mastering the playbook
sets you up to master the game.

MASTER THE GAME

To become a champion, you must "learn to conquer." This is usually a two-step process. First, you need to learn the rules of the game. These are often the official rules governing a specific activity at your school or in your sport. Learn what it takes to win or complete each activity properly so you don't lose all your hard work through disqualification or not doing it right from the start. Second, beyond learning the basic rules or plays in the playbook, you also need to learn how to conquer "the system" continually. In other words, figure out how to win or perform well at an activity on a consistent basis. This requires developing the skills, attitudes, habits, and plans to use both the official rules and the unofficial rules strategically to come out on top consistently. This is really how you tap into your true potential and separate yourself from the pack.

Whatever you face in college, you should always learn the ground rules so you can master the game. There are different types of rules—official, unofficial, spoken, unspoken, and written—that can be learned by reading, observing, and asking questions. The importance of learning these rules applies to everything on and off the field, including your studies, your athletics, and your personal life. When you master the playbook, you become more successful and have an advantage, no matter what you attempt.

___

ONE-ON-ONE

- **What does "ignorance is not bliss" mean for you as a student-athlete in the NCAA?**

- **Name some of the organizations or individuals whose rules you have to follow.**

- List some benefits of knowing and following the rules.

- What are three ways you can learn the rules?

- What do you need to learn to "master the game"?

GET READY TO SPRINT

Although I was a good student in high school and one of the best athletes for my age in the world, initially no one recruited me. Amazing, right? Rather than being discouraged or waiting for a recruiting call that might never come, I took the initiative and called the coach at one of the colleges I wanted to attend. Before that first telephone conversation, he knew nothing about me, but I had done my homework. For instance, I already knew that he had coached the NCAA champion in the 100- and 200-meter dashes the previous year. As we kept in contact during the next few months, I tried to convince him to give me an athletic scholarship even though he had never met me in person or seen me compete. I persisted, and finally I succeeded.

I learned early in my life about the importance of being proactive, which means having a goal in mind and then taking the necessary actions to reach that goal. From my first step onto campus as a freshman, I chose to be a go-getter. I was on a mission to reach specific goals and to create history, and I was determined that nothing would stop me. My top priorities were earning a college degree and winning an NCAA championship. Of course, I also wanted to show all those coaches who had not recruited me that they had dropped the ball.

At only seventeen, I understood that my success rested in my own hands. Although I had a great support team at home, the responsibility for my life and success in college lay on my shoulders. Although I was naïve and uncertain about many things, including how exactly I could pull it off, I knew for sure that success took hard work, sacrifice, commitment, and good plans.

Most people who consistently fail tend to lack initiative because they are not go-getters. They usually react to circumstances and other people. Instead of being proactive about achieving their goals, they wait until they are forced to do something on their own, such as when they are about to become academically ineligible or when they face a potentially season-ending injury because they did not visit the training room as they should have.

Champion student-athletes constantly fight for their successes from the start. They also respond to problems, circumstances, or other people properly by doing what they need to do quickly and decisively. They do not passively watch their lives unfold or always need prodding from others.

Many people know what they need to do and have good intentions but never follow through.

REALITY CHECK:
You are proactive about what matters most to you every day.

For example, you might actively work to manipulate circumstances so you "coincidentally" cross paths with someone you want to meet or see, like an attractive girl or guy at a party. You may actively try to avoid someone you don't want to run into, such as a friend to whom you owe $20 when you don't have it. In both of these cases, you act to achieve your goals because passively allowing "fate" to unfold is not good enough for you. This is the essence of being proactive. The true challenge is ensuring that you remain proactive about what *really* matters most as a student-athlete.

ACCESS YOUR RESOURCES

Even the most successful people sometimes need to seek help because they know that no single person has all the answers or resources. You will find that when you start to reach out, people tend to reach back and help you. Sometimes others may not immediately respond how you want them to, but if you remain respectful and determined, they will usually come around. Learn to use and leverage whatever goodwill you receive—as a representative of your school, a member of an organization, or a person—to your full advantage and stay open to new ideas. Don't tune out or reject good advice because you don't like when or how it was given or the person who gave it. Remember, a good idea is a good idea, regardless of the timing or source.

Make good use of your school and your own personal resources to help you reach your goals and true potential. These "resources" include your family, friends, teammates, coaches, counselors, staff members, classmates, and mentors. Each of these can play different but integral roles in your success.

Family usually comes first in our lives for good reasons. They tend to offer financial, emotional, and spiritual support because they usually have your best interests at heart. I underappreciated my family until I was in college. Even though they were always there for me, I did not stay in contact or rely on them as I should have during my first few months away from home. I was naturally a loner, and sometimes I felt too proud to ask them for help or to burden them when I was struggling. That changed after I finally reached out to them during some tough times. Their love and support helped me through those difficult periods and caused me to wonder why I had not allowed them to play a bigger role in my college life sooner. I don't know your family history or its current dynamics, but I strongly suggest that, if possible, you allow your family to be involved in your student-athlete experience from early on and in a meaningful way.

Friends may provide encouragement and guidance in various circumstances, such as during challenges in your romantic relationships. Or they may make your daily life easier in different ways, such as taking you to a grocery store or dropping you off at an appointment when you don't have a car. They can help you stay grounded and headed in the right direction when you start to lose focus. Good friends usually help you feel less lonely and share the ups and downs of life with you.

As an athlete, try to learn as much as possible from *teammates* about training and competing. Watch their techniques, strategies, and habits, particularly if they have more experience and skill than you do.

At first, adjusting to the intensity of my college workouts was difficult because I trained only three or four days a week in high school, and those sessions were relatively easy. For example, at the end of my first track workout in college, I had cramps all over, including my hamstrings, calves, neck, and back. It was the fall semester, and I had never before trained in weather so cold and windy. I probably vomited six or seven times too, including once in the training room and several other times on my disoriented and painful fifteen-minute walk back to my dorm room. I clearly remember thinking that I was going to pass out. Fortunately, over the next few months, I learned how to train harder and smarter, thanks to my teammates.

My teammates that year were not only talented but also highly competitive hard workers with winning attitudes. For instance, I recall a practice session in which one of my teammates was pushed from the track onto the grass infield by another teammate because he was running too slowly during one of their intervals. Also, I cannot tell you how much my teammates' praise and threats to me about performing well, particularly in our relay events, motivated me to do well in competitions. Much of what I learned from them during that first year, such as making my training count, setting high goals, competing without fear, and peaking when it mattered most, set the groundwork for me to win championships later in my career.

Teammates might also provide you with useful information about your courses and professors. For example, a teammate's advice about a tough professor's pet peeves helped me to do well in a course, while most of my classmates without this "inside" information struggled to pass. Good teammates also usually have your back in tough situations and try to help you fit in.

Besides discussing sports-related topics, *coaches* can offer insights on current problems and even career guidance. Experienced coaches usually tell many stories about their former athletes and competitions. As well as helping you to develop athletically, these stories may have positive life lessons that you can use during and after college.

Many days before training, I would go into my coach's office to hang out and chat. During those ten- or fifteen-minute visits, we spoke about almost everything from sports to personal issues. However, it was not always that easy for me to do, especially at the end of my first year when being injured and suffering burnout caused my performances to tank. Instead of encouraging me as my high school coach did when I was down, I felt that he had given up on me for the season at the most important time, during the Conference and NCAA Championships. I also thought that he had failed to deliver on some promises he made before I came to college. I know that many student-athletes feel this way about promises that their coaches made to them before they came to college.

At that time, I felt so down that I considered transferring to another school, but my father advised me to give the program another year. I don't think that my coach ever knew how frustrated I was because I made a conscious effort to build our relationship during my sophomore year. That was one of my best decisions in college. Over time, many of my coach's lessons helped me to become a better athlete and person.

Sometimes developing a good relationship with coaches can be challenging. For instance, they may have poor interpersonal skills or little interest in getting "too chummy" with their athletes. Because of the size of their teams or their schedules, they may be unable to have quality one-on-one time with each athlete. Still, try to develop relationships with them and to learn as much from them as you can. Always be respectful toward your coaches and *never* cross coach-athlete boundaries.

Academic advisors and *career counselors* can help you make better-informed choices about your academics or your post-collegiate career. Academic advisors work with you in making decisions from arranging class schedules to choosing a major. They might suggest ways to improve academically, such as enrolling in tutoring sessions or changing your study habits. They can also help you with postgraduate opportunities and options to finish your degree if your eligibility ends before you graduate. Career counselors offer advice and tools that are particularly useful for when you finally enter the workforce. These tools include enhancing your interviewing skills, résumé writing, and job search techniques. Your school's career services center may host career fairs, provide access to job opportunities, or even suggest potential employers.

Be proactive and talk with your *professors* and other *teaching staff* about grades and course requirements. They might give you tips or extra credit assignments to help you improve your grades. They usually are impressed when student-athletes have positive attitudes and take steps to improve in the classroom. Most schools also have some form of tutoring for those who need or want academic help. For example, teams constantly on the road, such as basketball, baseball, and volleyball teams, tend to have traveling tutors. Tutoring can be a great way to help you understand or master a subject.

Most *classmates* will gladly help you because many secretly wish that they were in your shoes—playing collegiate sports. They may, for instance, be good study partners or give you copies of their notes when you miss classes. Take advantage of their willingness to help, but do not abuse their goodwill.

Many successful people had *mentors* to help guide them during important stages of their development. Similarly, you can benefit from having a good mentor who offers wisdom, experience, and knowledge. Good mentors don't need to be famous, rich, or highly successful. Besides teaching or explaining, they listen to you with a genuine concern for you as a person. As a result, you can trust them to be honest with you about important and personal matters.

A good mentor challenges you to move beyond your excuses, limitations, and fears and to dig deep inside to reach your true potential. A mentor may volunteer to help you, or you may have to identify and ask someone to become your mentor. Just ensure that the person is willing, mature, and trustworthy and shows a genuine interest in your development. If you have never had a mentor before, you might find the adjustment of someone in your "space" or "face" somewhat awkward or difficult. However, for this relationship to work, you need to have the right attitude and become "mentorable." This means being respectful, humble, accountable, consistent, and willing to learn and try new things in order to become better—even when it's not easy.

In college, I had a few important mentors, mainly from my local church. They constantly challenged and encouraged me to do better, sometimes as an athlete, mostly as a person. Over time, they became like a second family to me. They had my back when I needed it most and were not afraid to "call me out" when I was not thinking or acting as I should have. Although I earned more accolades than they had, I still greatly respected their input and role in my personal growth. My success in college and my passion and ability to mentor others have much to do with their influence on my life.

YOU'VE GOT THE POWER, SO USE IT

Despite your circumstances, you always have the power to exercise your own free will. Sometimes your options may appear to be limited, less than ideal, or not obvious, but even in such cases you can still choose to act. In fact, choosing to do nothing in a circumstance is still a willful act. Applying this knowledge—that you can exercise your free will to make choices and determine your fate—moves you from reactivity and passivity to activity. Instead of simply reacting to situations, always work to create the best conditions so you can achieve your highest goals.

Be proactive about hitting your targets rather than waiting on others or the perfect conditions before you move forward. In other words, let who you want to be, where you want to go, and what you want to do become your main motivations to act. Being proactive plays a huge role in how your future unfolds.

Being proactive helps you to

- Avoid troublesome circumstances.
- Use your resources better.
- Maximize your personal potential.
- Increase your technical and life skills.
- Enjoy greater control over your life.
- Gain more personal satisfaction from your choices.

ENABLE YOURSELF

Perhaps the three main reasons student-athletes miss opportunities and fail to develop to their full potential while in college are laziness, feelings of self-entitlement, and negative enablers. Many student-athletes enter college expecting special treatment. They believe that the world should fall at their feet once they are athletes. In exchange for delivering outstanding athletic performances, or for just being on the team, they expect to be chauffeured down easy street.

Laziness—In simple terms, laziness is willfully choosing not to exert yourself. In other words, it means you're unwilling to do what you can or should be doing. It usually stems from feeling overconfident or having low personal interest in an activity. Being lazy has no benefits but potentially many drawbacks. For example, not regularly working on your goals because of laziness will eventually lead you off course and maybe even into trouble. Like a disease, laziness can become contagious if not dealt with properly, spreading from one part of your life to another.

REALITY CHECK:
Laziness leads to poor choices and subpar results because you are being a minimalist, taking shortcuts, or playing catch-up. Poor results as a student-athlete can cause you unnecessary academic or athletic problems.

Lazy student-athletes constantly have reasons why they are not more diligent about taking care of their business. They tend to blame circumstances or others for why they don't do better. Champion student-athletes, on the other hand, take personal responsibility for outcomes in their lives. They discipline themselves to keep doing what they should be doing at the right time and in the right way. This becomes particularly obvious when they feel less motivated or face tougher challenges.

Self-entitlement—How many times have you seen certain student-athletes strut around campus acting as though everyone should bow down when they pass? Their actions and attitudes often reflect an inner belief that they deserve preferential treatment because of their athletic accomplishments or because of "who they are." They view help from others as their right and expect special benefits whether rightfully earned or not. This warped view often causes them to avoid hard work and sacrifice when it matters most. They tend to look for the easiest route and constantly expect friends, teammates, staff, or others to do things for them. Some even expect others to keep them eligible!

During my freshman year, I had many highly motivated and hard working teammates. We wanted to be the best, and we succeeded in becoming one of the top programs in the nation. After that season, things changed because most of the hardest working athletes on the team were seniors whose eligibility ended. Although many incoming new teammates were also talented, some entered the program with the wrong attitudes. Instead of earning respect the old-fashioned way—through their performance or conduct—they expected special treatment or privileges before they even scored a point for the school.

As cocaptain, I had to deal with how their sense of entitlement negatively affected team chemistry. For instance, some childishly gossiped and complained so much about what our team ("they") didn't have that it started to rub off on other teammates who had no real problems with our program. Apparently those complainers thought that just being on the roster entitled them to some special treatment regardless of their performance, attitude, or behavior. Wrong! Ironically, the ones who seemed to want the most special treatment often had the poorest work ethics and the weakest performances at competitions. If they had spent more time working hard and focusing on handling their own business, instead of expecting to be pampered and spoon-fed, they would have earned more respect and become more successful.

Negative enablers—Because you are a student-athlete, some people will offer you help, especially if you are a star athlete or play a particular sport. Getting help can make your life easier, particularly when you have a busy schedule or if you struggle in an area. However, if you are not willing to do your own hard work, you can start to rely on others too much. Be careful in these situations. While most people offer legitimate and positive help, others' assistance can be negative. I call these people "negative enablers."

"Positive enablers" offer you support when you are weak or overwhelmed in some area, such as a classmate who offers to become a tutor or study partner in a course that you may be failing. Positive enablers intend to help and empower you to work through challenges to reach your goal. Occasionally, they may do some "heavy lifting" for you, but they still expect you to do most of the hard work. In contrast, negative enablers discourage you from being proactive by constantly doing for you what you should be doing on your own, such as a classmate who decides to write a term paper or take an exam for you. Rather than helping you develop self-reliance and personal responsibility, negative enablers often encourage bad habits, bad attitudes, and bad conduct.

You can struggle at times to identify negative enablers, determine their motives, and see how they harm you. For example, negative enablers can range from people you barely know, like fans or boosters, to those close to you, like family members or coaches. Some may help in order to boost their own relationship with you or to ensure that you remain eligible to compete. Others may care for you so much that they unintentionally become negative enablers. They move from supporting you to harming you by discouraging you—directly or indirectly—from properly dealing with important issues in your life.

We all need help to improve, reach higher goals, and get through difficult circumstances, but we need help from the right people, at the right time, and in the right way. Negative enablers have helped ruin many lives, including several celebrities and sportspeople. Although you cannot avoid them entirely, you can perhaps limit their negative influences on you. Be wary of "yes" people in your life and those who don't "check" you when you should or could do better.

REALITY CHECK:
Laziness, self-entitlement, and negative enablers rob you of the chance to learn many important lessons and skills needed to advance your own ball down the field successfully in college and beyond.

This may not seem like a big deal now, but it is. Not only are you giving others significant control of your future, you are also setting yourself up for failure because you don't prepare properly for life when those people are not around or they cannot help you.

A good friend of mine got a rare opportunity to redeem himself in a course that he was about to fail. Because he was a student-athlete, his professor gave him another chance to pass the class by allowing him to hand in an extra credit paper before final grades. However, my friend had already made plans to visit a girl out of town for a weekend. Saddled with this dilemma, he approached some teammates for help. Finally, his team's equipment manager came to his rescue. The next day, the equipment manager gave him a copy of an essay from his extensive stash of previously used papers. Even with this "hookup," my friend asked another teammate to retype the paper for him. This teammate refused and told him to stop being so lazy and to carry his own weight.

With time rapidly slipping away, my friend made a crucial choice—he sped out to the nearest copy store. Because he wanted to head to the airport for his weekend rendezvous, he asked yet another teammate to hand in the paper for him. (See a trend yet?) This time, his teammate agreed and did a quick scan of the essay. To his horror and amusement, he realized that my friend had photocopied the entire paper—including the professor's final grade and comments in the margins! The teammate refused to hand it in that way, certainly not with the original final grade at the end. Never short of "tricks," my friend crookedly tore off the bottom of that page by hand and bolted through the door to catch his plane.

Although he was talented and successful in his sport, he allowed his professor, teammates, and even his equipment manager to act as negative enablers to him. Of course, he failed that course and continued to struggle academically for the rest of his college career because he was not proactive about improving in the classroom.

THE WORLD OWES YOU NOTHING

One of the most influential comments my father ever made to me was that the world owed me nothing. At first, I felt upset because I was facing a tough situation and wanted his support, but after a few days, I realized that what he said was correct. He basically meant that my abilities, accomplishments, or status did not automatically obligate others to respond how I wanted them to. I needed to exert myself and be proactive about my choices in life, even when others did not respect or support me as I thought they should have. I also realized that I should never give other people enough power to stop me from acting

During the next few years, my motivation increased significantly. My father and others continued to help and encourage me, but much of my success came from my desire to excel and not shirk, panhandle for special favors, or regularly allow negative enablers to influence my choices. Even though my personal faith deeply influenced me, I did not believe in allowing my life to unfold passively. Patience was important, but also I realized that if I simply sat back, stopped working, and waited for the "right" circumstances or people to come, or if I allowed the opinions, attitudes, and actions of others toward me determine my fate, then key opportunities would pass me by. I needed to be involved in my success all day, every day. I preferred to try and fail rather than fail because I did not try.

Regardless of your accomplishments, who you are, or your background, the world really owes *you* nothing. Accepting this will either cause you to quit or inspire you to "go for it."

REALITY CHECK:
If you are not prepared to be a
go-getter, don't expect to excel or
separate yourself from the pack.

BE PRACTICALLY PROACTIVE

In practical terms, being proactive means voluntarily staying on top of important matters like your classes, bills, personal issues, and injuries *before* troubles arise or others have to push you along. Being proactive also involves getting the right help from the right people at the right time and ensuring that you keep doing your part *before* trouble comes knocking at your door. Remember, getting into trouble as a student-athlete can be costly, so try to avoid it.

However, avoiding trouble is not always possible. In such cases, you should continue to value and protect your future and realize that you still have free will to make choices, even when you have few alternatives. Rather than passively watching your life unfold or allowing others to decide your fate, try to work on resolving the matter as soon as possible. Don't compound your trouble by using an illegal or inappropriate fix. Avoid more hassles by doing it the right way. This might entail working out plans with your professors, coaches, or advisors or maybe taking the first step to repair a strained relationship.

Whatever your goals, prepare to take the initiative and follow through until you reach them. Being proactive will help you to develop greater self-reliance and personal responsibility—two important life skills that always affect your success.

Remember, if someone cares more about your business than you do, you need to "check" yourself and become more proactive about your life. Push hard and sprint toward your future.

ONE-ON-ONE

- **What does being proactive mean to you?**

- **How has being proactive influenced your success?**

- **What are four resources that you can access and how can they benefit you?**

- **What roles have laziness, feelings of self-entitlement, and negative enablers played in your life and why?**

- **What steps can you take to fix some things in your academic, athletic, or personal life?**

IMPROVE YOUR PERSONAL GOALKEEPING

On the weekend before the Outdoor Conference Champion-ships in my freshman year, I suffered a severe injury. Earlier that season, I had set a world record for my age group, and most people were impressed with how well I had performed all year. As an eighteen-year-old world record-holder, I felt a tremendous amount of pressure to perform near that world record standard all the time, even while injured. Unfortunately the combination of the injury plus not adjusting my high personal expectations caused me to perform worse during championship season and to lose self-confidence. Ultimately a timely reality check and some advice from a sports psychologist helped me to get back on the right track.

That session motivated me to reevaluate my goal-setting habits and look more carefully at how they affected my performances and me. For instance, were my goals causing me to feel so stressed when I competed that I forced my performances rather than let everything flow? Or were they unreasonable based on my abilities, history, current circumstances, or resources? I spent more time determining whether my goals were indeed realistic, healthy, and useful. I had to ask myself whether people truly expected me to deliver a world record performance all the time or whether I simply projected my personal expectations and values onto others. This was deep stuff for an eighteen-year-old, but this process changed how I thought about my goals. I want to share with you some of what I learned along the way.

YOU CAN'T WIN WHEN YOU'RE GOAL-LESS

I cannot tell you how many times I witnessed teammates and fellow student-athletes go through semester after semester and season after season without properly setting and pursuing personal goals. Without proper goals, you will fail to live up to your potential, and you can get caught up with many nonessential activities of college life.

REALITY CHECK:
You simply cannot afford not to have proper goals because you have too much at stake and your time as a student-athlete decreases with every passing moment.

Setting and working toward personal goals are important keys to success, in sports and beyond. Perhaps I am preaching to the choir since you probably already know this. You cannot become a collegiate student-athlete if, at some stage, you don't have some success setting and reaching your goals. To be consistently successful in college, you must learn how to perfect these skills to avoid falling prey to mediocrity and distraction.

Perhaps you noticed my emphasis on setting *and* working toward goals. People can talk or daydream forever about what they want to do, but how many consistently work toward achieving those goals? The combination of constantly setting and pursuing personal goals is a powerful life skill and increases the likelihood that you will achieve the success that you want.

It is essential that you take the time to define what success in college means to you—what goals you want to accomplish academically, sportswise, and in your personal life before your eligibility ends; in other words, what "life moments" or achievements you want during your college career. Personal goals go beyond the expectations others have for you, but your goals will often be similar to those of others, such as your coaches, parents, teammates, and professors. Although their goals may guide you, you should still set your own. For instance, coaches always want you to do well in your academics and athletics, but it is far more important for those to be your personal goals because you are the main one responsible for achieving them and living with your results. The more thought you give to setting and determining what you need to do in order to reach your goals, the better your results will likely be.

SUCCESS TIPS FOR SETTING AND REACHING YOUR GOALS

Here are six basic questions, sometimes called the "6Ws" of goal setting, that can help you to make proper goals:

- *Who*—Who is involved? Are you the main person or part of a team effort?
- *What*—What specifically do you want to achieve?
- *Where*—Define the location of the goal. Does this include one location or more?

- *When*—Set the time frame. Will it be short-term, intermediate, or long-term? Does it involve one or more occasions?
- *Which*—Determine the requirements and challenges of reaching your objectives. Which resources do you need? Are they accessible to you? Will you need help, and if so whose help?
- *Why*—What reasons drive you to pursue the goal?

Carefully consider and write down your answers before you commit your time and resources to an important goal. Bear in mind that sometimes you may need a few days to research or to clarify some information before you can answer all these questions properly. The better you can answer these questions, the better your goals will be.

KEEP IT REAL

When your goals align with your character and core beliefs, your journey becomes easier, although not necessarily easy. You will experience less internal conflict and higher self-motivation and contentment if what you want to achieve is consistent with your personal values. On the other hand, when you go against your convictions and character, you may still hit your targets, but inwardly the process will become more challenging and less fulfilling. For example, you can make an illegal but hard-to-detect play against a competitor in order to win or cheat on an exam to pass a course. What should you do? Winning competitions and passing your courses are important but not at the expense of your integrity. Remember, when you reach your goal, you also will have to live with the consequences of how you reached it.

GET SPECIFIC

Specifically "what?"—How often have you heard people claim to know what they want, yet they cannot "find the right words" to explain it? If you press them to define what they mean more precisely, they really can't do it. More likely than not, they have not yet achieved consistent success in that area. If you can't express your goals in clear terms, then you will have trouble reaching them. You always stand a better chance of reaching specific targets instead of general ones if you can state them simply and clearly.

For example, like most students, you probably want to do well in school. Does that mean getting an A, B, or C in your classes? Be specific about what goals you want to reach. Specific goals focus your thoughts and actions and help you to avoid the drift that comes from trying to achieve vague targets.

REALITY CHECK:
As a student-athlete, you simply don't
have the luxury of being carefree or coasting
to an unknown or poorly defined destination.
You need to hit certain specific targets
in the classroom and on the playing
field to maintain your status.

Having specific objectives also allows you to involve the right people for reaching your goals. You don't have to be an eloquent speaker or make a PowerPoint presentation, but you should be able to tell others what you want in clear terms. This clarity will help when planning your strategy and coordinating whatever resources you need. After you have identified your objectives, make them clear, brief, and simple, perhaps putting them in bullet point format. You will make them a lot easier to remember and to express to others. I recommend that for important goals or those for which you will need help from others, you spend more time refining your answers to the "6Ws." If you can clearly answer those questions, then you will probably be able to articulate clearly your goals and the plans to reach them to others.

Specifically "when?"—All your goals should also have a specific time frame. Setting a definite time frame allows you to judge your progress more objectively and helps you to determine when you need to make adjustments. Three basic time frames fit most goals—short-term, intermediate, and long-term.

Short-term goals are those that you want to accomplish in the near future, such as in a day, a week, or perhaps a couple of months. Those might include what you want to achieve during your regular workouts or the number of chapters you want to read from your textbook in an evening. Intermediate goals, such as reaching a certain training level by the end of your preseason, lie somewhere between your short-term and long-term goals. Long-term goals usually require more background work, such as aiming to become a finalist at your conference championships. Time frames for goals may also be interrelated or overlap. For instance, you may want to earn a B in a particular class as your short-term goal, to finish the semester with a 3.0 GPA as your intermediate goal, and to graduate in four years as your long-term goal.

REALITY CHECK:
Timeless goals are seldom completed properly or by when they could be the most effective.

Writing down your goals and their deadlines and displaying them help you to remember your top priorities. The more you revisit them, the more they stick in your mind and positively influence your commitment and actions. As a matter of habit, write them on something that you cannot easily destroy or misplace and keep them where you can constantly access and see them. Many athletes write their athletic goals on their equipment, such as their shoes or helmets, or in places that they will frequently have to pass, like their bathroom mirrors. I wrote my athletic goals in my training journal and sometimes I even made them my passwords or personal identification numbers (PINs). Some coaches display team goals prominently at the team's practice facility or in team locker rooms. These serve as constant visual reminders of the team's specific destination and ways of reaching it. You should do the same with your academics, athletics, and other aspects of your life.

Writing down my bigger goals helped to remind me of my original intentions. Sometimes those goals seemed impossible to reach, such as when I had drifted far from the right path or after a particularly bad performance or series of subpar ones. However, those goals did not seem so "crazy" after visually reinforcing and repeating them aloud to myself on a regular basis. I found that the combination of seeing my handwriting and hearing my own voice positively affirmed and greatly boosted my confidence in my abilities. It shifted my attention away from what I may not have done well or a current negative circumstance toward what I believed was possible for me to do when I started my journey.

When creating a personal timeline for your goals in college, make sure you use three primary resources: your class syllabuses, your competition schedule, and the NCAA progress-toward-degree requirements. Your timeline should always coincide with important dates in all those schedules. Give yourself enough time to prepare properly for whatever activities are scheduled on those dates so that you can do well at what matters most.

MAKE SURE IT MEASURES UP

Besides being specific and set within a time frame, goals need to be measurable. If you cannot measure your goals as you go along, you will not know whether you are going in the right direction or at the right pace or whether you need to make adjustments. Set goals that you can frequently and easily track, rather than waiting until the end to find out if you stayed on target. Suppose you aim to earn a B in one of your courses. Not only do you have a definite goal, but you can also measure your progress throughout the semester by your performance in exams and other graded activities, like papers, pop quizzes, and group projects. Before the semester ends, you will have an idea of your progress and whether you must make some changes to earn the grade you want.

Picking a goal like "I want to feel better about myself" presents a challenge that may not at first be obvious. Although you have a good idea, you cannot objectively measure your progress. Wanting to feel better about yourself might mean feeling more self-confident, improving your physical health, or developing into a more giving person. All these possibilities can result from the goal of feeling better about yourself, so which one is it? If you choose a goal that you cannot definitely measure, you can't objectively know how you are progressing or, sometimes, when you have reached it.

During my longer runs in training, I asked my coach or one of the assistants to shout out my time at equal intervals. I always wanted to hear my intermediate split times so that I would know if I was on the right pace or if I needed to accelerate or slow down to reach the target time. I could then train smarter and with greater consistency, which helped me to make the most of my coach's workout program for me by avoiding overtraining or undertraining.

Having measurable goals reduces guesswork, allows you to monitor your progress, and lets you know whether you have hit your target. It helps you to find your personal rhythm of doing things and often gives you the opportunity to make whatever changes are needed to reach your intermediate and final objectives before it's too late. Choosing measurable targets allows you to set up more meaningful plans to reach them.

ADAPT AND ACT

If you hope to improve in any area, your goals must challenge you to develop and give more of yourself to reach them, but they still need to be realistic. You can save yourself from unnecessary embarrassment, frustration, disappointment, or even injury by avoiding unreachable objectives from the start. For example, deciding that you want to write a major term paper in two days, when you really should give yourself several weeks for researching, typing, and proofing it properly, sets you up for problems.

REALITY CHECK:
Unattainable goals drain you of
time, energy, and resources—all limited
commodities for a student-athlete.

Make a fair assessment of your performance history, skills, habits, resources, and challenges. If you do not have the time, abilities, or opportunities to reach your goals, then they are probably unrealistic and need to be changed.

No one hits his goals all the time. If someone says that he does, he is lying, has incredibly low goals, or both. Revising your goals does not mean that you have waved the white flag of surrender and quit. For example, unfavorable circumstances that you had not expected might sometimes force you to adjust your plans. Several times throughout my career I had to do this because of injuries to my teammates or me, but I never just quit because I could not reach my original targets in the time or way I wanted.

For instance, during my senior year, I contracted chicken pox immediately following the indoor season. Even though my immune system had not properly recovered, I forced myself back into action a few weeks later. Bad idea. I got injured at my first outdoor competition because my body was too weak to perform at that level. Even though I knew this from my workouts some days before, I ignored it and convinced my coach that I could still compete. I had already missed many days of training because of the chicken pox, and I was scared of falling behind and not finally winning the NCAA Outdoor Championships titles that had eluded me my entire career.

In the following days, the reality of still being weak from the chicken pox virus, newly injured, and about two months away from the end of my college career struck me hard. In fact, I almost cried one afternoon while walking across the infield on the way to talk to my coach about everything. (I probably cried fewer than five times in my entire career over anything sports-related, so that was major for me.) Thankfully, the stadium was empty!

During that meeting, I finally surrendered to the fact that I needed to become more flexible about my goals for the season. I needed to make new and realistic goals that took my setbacks into consideration. For example, instead of obsessing about the "big picture"—winning the national championship—

regaining my health became the top priority. That meant patiently waiting for the virus to clear my system and staying on top of daily rehab on my injured hamstring. Training smarter took the place of participating in certain competitions that originally were supposed to be my prechampionship warm-ups and benchmarks. By focusing on completing my revised and more realistic goals properly, I slowly worked myself back into shape. Because I did not simply give up out of discouragement, what seemed unlikely only two months before became a reality: I ended my college career on the top of the podium at the NCAA Outdoor Championships.

Staying flexible allows you to make the most of your circumstances—favorable or unfavorable—and keep working when conditions change.

You will need to work with others to reach many of your goals. Be clear about your purpose and agree on expectations with everyone involved to reduce potential conflicts and make the most of your working relationships. This principle applies whether you deal with teammates, classmates in a group project, or people in your personal relationships. It especially applies with your coach. For example, suppose you and your coach have vastly different goals for the season, like what position you should play or what events you should enter. At some stage, conflict will arise between the two of you, and chances are you will come out the loser, unless you both come to a mutual agreement about priorities and roles.

Setting clear expectations at the start about roles, responsibilities, and plans will help you avoid misunderstandings as well as wasting time and energy. Don't let egos and personal issues get in the way of reaching your goals. Let others' strengths supplement your weaknesses and stay open-minded to ideas and alternatives that can help you to reach your targets more easily or more effectively.

Remember, you need to act, not just make goals. For example, you might want to raise your GPA from 2.8 to 3.2 in the next semester or place in the top three in your next competition—but that's not enough. Although writing down these goals and giving yourself regular reminders about them are good habits, you have to move beyond the intellectual process and be proactive about achieving your targets. This may include revamping your study habits and finding a tutor or coming to training more focused over the next few weeks.

Worthwhile goals always require action. Setting goals is the easy part, but following through until the end makes the difference.

KEEP UP YOUR TARGET PRACTICE

Try to set goals for everything you do. You don't need to wait for a big task. Smaller or short-term goals often help you to achieve greater ones later. Try to reach as many of your objectives—small or big—as possible. The more you practice hitting your targets, the more self-confidence you will gain. You will also improve your goal-setting and goal-reaching strategies in general, which are valuable assets for college and the rest of your life.

Not all goals are equally important, so you should rank them in order of significance. Do not let less important or less immediate goals take priority over ones that are more important or pressing. Always take care of first things first.

I liked setting goals. In fact, I usually felt uneasy without goals and a set deadline. Without a clear objective, I felt unfocused, wasted time, and accomplished less. In other words, my mind drifted, time got away, and my productivity went down. I tried to set goals for almost everything I did, from my schoolwork to my athletics. For example, in spite of my course load or competition season, I started each semester with the aim of earning a 4.0 GPA; as they say, I shot for the stars. This remained my number one priority all semester—superseding even my athletic goals. I made sacrifices and approached each exam and assignment with this overarching objective in mind—to earn an A. I missed this ambitious goal in each of my first four semesters by one course, but by my junior year, I figured out the secrets to doing it.

I was also extremely goal oriented in my athletics. My seasonal goals were ambitious but relatively few and specific. For example, in the short term I usually set goals for each workout session based on what my coach wanted me to execute that day, on how I felt, and on what I thought needed attention. My intermediate goals were to perfect my race model and to qualify for the NCAA Championships in my events at specific competitions during the season. Winning those events at the Conference and NCAA Championships were my long-term objectives. Academically, completing my short-term goals, such as reviewing notes from lectures on a daily basis and doing my homework on time, allowed me to accomplish my intermediate goals, like doing well on exams and papers, in turn making my long-term goal of getting an A in a course possible.

As you can see, how well I completed my short-term and intermediate goals influenced my ability to reach my long-term ones. The attention I paid to hitting targets in my daily workouts allowed me to develop the tools needed to execute good performances at my prechampionship competitions. These solid performances not only helped me to perfect my competition tactics and qualify for the NCAA Championships but also boosted my self-confidence. Using goals to develop the proper skills, strategies, and self-confidence made it easier for me to perform at my best when it mattered most.

Setting and pursuing proper, realistic, and specific goals allowed me to focus my actions, time, and resources throughout each semester. These goals were constant guides and motivators that helped me to build a successful student-athlete career. They can do the same for you.

ONE-ON-ONE

- Why do you need proper goals in college?

- What happens when your goals are not consistent with your core values and beliefs?

- What six questions should you consider when making a goal?

- Can you list three specific goals that you have as a student, an athlete, and a person? What time frame do you have for each of those goals?

- Why might you need to be flexible and change a goal?

PERFECT YOUR PERSONAL
GAME PLAN

When I did experiments in my high school science labs, I learned that I could create a small ecosystem with a few plants, dirt, and other elements in a terrarium. If I wanted to repeat those results, I needed consistency in my method. I also discovered that I could predict changes in results based on changes in the system. A light went on for me. If "systemization" worked in the lab, maybe it could work for me too.

I knew that the older I got, the harder my schoolwork and competitions would become, but I would still have the same amount of time each day to prepare. I needed a consistent way to improve in my studies and athletics if I were going to earn an athletic scholarship. I thought about it some more and started developing a useful personal system. For example, I created a regular study routine by using some tips I learned one summer from reading a book about effective study habits. I also developed routines for my athletics, including my warm-up and how I approached my training and competitions.

My interest in the different ways that people achieved success also grew.

REALITY CHECK:
The "great ones"—whether musicians, artists, scientists, or athletes—use systematic approaches to their crafts. Even though the specific actions needed to do well in each discipline might vary, many of the ideas, attitudes, and habits underlying their success are similar.

You already have a systematic way of going about daily tasks such as getting yourself ready in the morning and preparing for training or classes. In fact, everyone uses a personal system of some sort. Creating your own "game plan" means that you develop a consistent, organized, and productive way of doing things. Instead of randomly changing how you do the same activity, you use a consistent pattern or structure. For instance, think about how you brush your teeth or how you prepare for a competition. One of your main goals as a student-athlete should be to develop a successful system for your academics, athletics, and personal life.

One of my toughest challenges was learning how to transfer my high school system to college. I had to make many changes because being a college student-athlete demanded more focus and time than anything I had ever experienced before. For example, unlike my high school workouts that lasted for no more than an hour and a half, practice in college was closer to three hours, including visiting the training room and lifting weights. I also had many more deadlines for schoolwork than I had in high school.

As a rule, I tried not to make random adjustments. Instead I thought hard about the potential effects of any change before I integrated it into my regular routine. Would it help or throw off other things I was doing or wanted to achieve? In the process of developing and trying out different routines, I discovered that I could often predict my range of results in exams and competitions based on my preparations, and I rarely performed lower than those projections. You too can learn to predict many of your performances through systemization just as I did.

I focused on achieving consistent results, and if an approach could not deliver the consistency I wanted, then I changed it. Results mattered most. I always wanted to see if I could produce the same or better results and take less time or feel less drained doing so. For example, every year I tweaked my approaches to studying and to training, mainly based on what I learned from previous years or seasons. Sometimes I found these adjustments useful, and other times I reverted to what had worked best in the past.

The greater the stakes, the more time I spent preparing in a consistent and methodical way. I tried not to leave much to chance, particularly in tough classes, when facing formidable competitors, or at championships. Being consistently systematic not only helped me to improve my knowledge and technical skills in an area but also boosted my self-confidence. My goal was to develop and practice the approaches that suited me the best because I knew that those routines gave me the best shot to do well.

As I developed my personal game plan, I also noticed that systematic approaches related to all sorts of situations. For example, you have probably noticed that some college programs are always successful in certain sports. Of course, many have sizable budgets, ample resources, and top recruits. If you look a little closer, you will see that beyond these elements, all these programs share something more important: They all use a systematic approach to succeed. Winning programs do well because they find and keep doing what works best for them—some people call this "tradition."

The same holds true for successful people in all walks of life. They know that lasting success rarely occurs by accident or luck. Success results from a combination of factors aligning at the right time and in the right way. By knowing what those factors are and understanding the conditions needed for them to work together to succeed in each activity you do, you can create an effective game plan to reach all your own goals.

Having a good "game plan"
- Helps organize, clarify, and simplify whatever you do.
- Creates less variance in your results.
- Increases confidence in your ability to reproduce results.
- Provides another useful tool for making self-assessments.

BECOME SYSTEMATICALLY SUCCESSFUL

Most coaches systematize; definitely the better ones do. For instance, they spend a lot of time and money trying to assess and recruit the best athletes to fit their programs. Coaches cannot afford to tolerate athletes who are negligent or carefree about matters as important as their schoolwork and athletics, even if those athletes have great athletic abilities. Most coaches also spend significant time preparing workouts, creating game strategies, and scheduling the right competitions for their teams. Poor systems for recruiting and preparing athletes produce the wrong mix of players on their rosters and increase the risk of injury and poor results.

In the NCAA, all coaches in the same sport must follow the same rules. Successful coaches find ways to get their players to achieve better results than their competitors. For example, they often make their players technically more efficient in their positions or events. They know that raising technical efficiency often leads to better overall performances with less fluctuation. Because players waste less energy per task, like shooting, running, jumping, blocking, or passing, they achieve more in the same amount of time or with less effort. Improved technical efficiency also reduces the likelihood of injuries and burnout. Good coaches also systematically develop their teams' skill sets so that their athletes can step up and play different positions or participate in different events when needed. All these provide a solid platform for a winning season.

Some colleges will fire coaches in revenue-earning sports if their systems consistently fail to deliver wins—even in the middle of the season. Similarly, if you use an ineffective system, you could be risking your financial aid, your role on the team, or even your eligibility to compete.

As a student-athlete, you need a good personal system to help you produce consistently good results, especially away from the field, which is perhaps the area where most student-athletes run into problems. Although your coach is responsible for creating and overseeing a system for you to develop as an athlete, most schools do not provide nearly as much structure for the development of student-athletes in their academic and personal lives. For instance, your coach may use mandatory checks like study hall and tutoring, class attendance monitors, or curfews, but most of these are basic measures to ensure that you handle your business and stay out of trouble. However, if you want to become more than average, then you must shoulder more personal responsibility and make better plans.

Actually, because you are a young adult, your school is *not* responsible for managing your life in areas such as your eating habits, your money, or your relationships.

REALITY CHECK:
If you don't consciously develop a proper system for your life, especially away from the field or classroom, you can easily and seriously go off course.

ONE SIZE DOES NOT FIT ALL

Sayings like "There is more than one way to skin a cat" and "More than one road leads to Rome" are popular because people recognize that many different paths may allow you to reach your goals.

REALITY CHECK:
Just because a system works for someone else does not mean that the same system will work best for you.

In other words, simply copying what others do is not enough to do well in college, regardless of who they are. For example, some students find studying earlier in the day to be more productive, but like me, you may find scheduling regular daytime study sessions less productive than studying in the evening. Your school may set up similar basic routines for all its student-athletes to follow, some of which may not be best suited for you.

Like all freshman student-athletes, I had to attend mandatory study hall for three or four nights a week during my first semester of college. I always struggled to stay focused during those times because it was like a social hour for all the student-athletes who had to be there. Although I understood the purpose of mandatory study hall—to ensure that freshmen and student-athletes with low grades did some daily structured studying—it did not work well for me. I developed my own routine in which I did my easy schoolwork during study hall and more demanding studies at another location and time, away from the talking and distractions of other student-athletes.

Of course, you should follow all mandatory rules but whenever allowed, do what works best for you. If you want to succeed across many areas of your life, you need to develop a personal system tailored to maximize your strengths, minimize your weaknesses, improve your performances, and reduce variations in your results.

QUICK TIPS FOR ENHANCING YOUR GOOD GAME PLAN

Developing a good game plan usually takes some time and much trial and error. Here are some tips that can fast-track this process:

- Identify people—alive or dead—whose achievements you most admire or want to emulate. They may be close to you, such as a family member or teammate, or people you don't know well or at all, like a competitor a professional athlete, or a businessperson.
- Identify what factors and conditions may have helped them to succeed. This could be as simple as directly questioning someone who is close or available to you, or it may require more time and effort, such as researching the Internet or library for quotes, interviews, articles, or biographies about the person.

Take note of what specific actions or approaches they used to overcome opponents or obstacles as well as their attitudes, motivations, and habits. Consider what circumstances apparently helped or hurt them, especially if they were successful many times or over long periods. Above all, try to find the basic principles on which they built their success.

- Compare the reasons for their success with the reasons for your past or current performances. Bear in mind that because of differences in your abilities and circumstances, you may not be able to emulate many of their specific actions or accomplishments. However, the attitudes, habits, and principles underlying their success may be useful in improving or getting more from your own game plan.

After you find a system that gives you positive results, continue to refine it to fit your specific needs. You may consider merging ideas from different experiences or sources such as TV programs and books, as well as working with your coaches, professors, and advisors to tweak a little here and there—bearing in mind that your game plan will never be perfect.

During preseason training, I usually tried to "negotiate" with my coach about adding some drills or exercises that worked for me in high school. (Trust me, it is not easy to get someone with over thirty years of experience coaching good athletes, including several NCAA champions, to accept these suggestions wholesale.) However, we did try to tweak many different ideas throughout my career, which helped me to improve as an athlete. Stay alert and open-minded because while fine-tuning, you might discover a better way to reach your goals. Remember, keep refining and practicing your personal game plan until you achieve your best results consistently.

AVOID EXTREME MAKEOVERS

Extreme makeovers may make good television, but they can disrupt your life. Changing too much too soon may backfire on you because your mind and body can lose their bearings and become out of sync, leading to worse results than gradually integrating changes into your personal system. I learned this lesson the hard way at a world championship a few years after I finished college.

Ten days before the start of my first event, I was in tremendous physical and mental shape. I was hungry to win, and my training was superb. My coach and trainers decided to change my diet radically to give me an extra edge when I competed. I agreed and began eating the healthiest diet I had ever eaten. This meant no more hamburgers and fries and very low sugar consumption. Although I competed well, I was still disappointed to finish fourth in my first event, especially since I was predicted to win a medal.

After another subpar performance in the semifinals of my second event, my coach, my trainers, and I felt confused. We all knew that something was not right, but we could not put our fingers on a solution. On the drive back to the hotel, I asked if the changes to my diet could be the answer. Suddenly, we all realized that perhaps my body had not known how to process all the healthy food properly during the past few days. We tried another radical approach in response. During the rest day between the semifinals and finals of that event, they tried to "restart" my system by going to the other extreme— forcing me to eat more junk food and sugar than usual. Too little, too late, and once more I finished disappointingly shy of the medals in the finals.

Although certain circumstances demand urgent and extreme changes for your immediate well-being, as a rule, gradual changes cause fewer problems than radical ones. In practical terms, that might mean increasing your daily study time from one hour to one and a half or two hours, rather than trying to jump immediately to three-hour daily study sessions. You will often adapt better when you give your mind and body time to adjust to changes instead of shocking or overloading them.

THE "FOUR Es" OF A GOOD PERSONAL SYSTEM

Regardless of what you do, where you get your ideas, or how you tweak them, if your personal system is going to give you the best, most consistent results, then it needs to have what I call the "Four Es." All good systems should be Effective, Efficient, Easily Repeatable, and Elastic.

Effective—Above all, a system must work. If it does not give you the results you want, then you have to change or discard it. You need an effective system that gives you the best results in the classroom, on the field, and beyond. For example, if your current study habits do not help you earn the grades that you want, then change the way you study. You might have to read a guide on developing good study habits or get extra tutoring. The same applies to athletics and your personal life. Remember, if you continue to do the same things in the same way, you achieve the same results. Having an effective system is a priority.

Efficient—As a student-athlete, you should also aim to streamline your activities by achieving greater efficiency. You can't afford to spend all day, every day on finishing one or two tasks. You simply have too many other duties to perform and almost always too little time to finish everything properly. By refining your system and improving your efficiency, you can achieve similar results but with more rest and more time at your disposal. Your system should help you to work smarter, not harder.

For example, on one evening you might have to read ten chapters for a class. If the assignment does not involve highly technical work, try skimming or scanning techniques, which allow you to cover material much faster than traditional word-for-word reading methods. Perhaps you can finish the ten chapters in two hours rather than three and a half hours. Although both methods achieve similar results, one allows you to finish sooner, thereby giving you more time to spend working on your other classes or a chance to go to bed earlier, which may help you to perform better on the next day. Aim for efficiency every day in everything you do—without cutting corners or cheating, of course.

Easily repeatable—If you want to make great improvements with your system, then it must be easily repeatable—something you can readily do over and over again. This means that it can work without constantly requiring special conditions or too much time or energy. Getting the results you want from your system may require hard work at first to get over the learning curve, but the process should become easier over time. Remember, you need a system that helps you produce on a daily basis in the classroom, on the field, and in other aspects of your life. If what you need to do to succeed is not easily repeatable, then your results will be inconsistent.

Elastic—Even with the best intentions and plans, things will not always go as planned. Your system needs to be flexible, not written in stone and capable of being changed. Elasticity allows you to continue working by making proper real-time adjustments under imperfect conditions. Although you hope for the best, you prepare for the worst.

Elasticity and flexibility are common characteristics of the game plans that most successful people use. They stand apart from others, in part, because their systems allow them to make productive real-time adjustments in less than ideal circumstances. Most people can get good results from their system when the "stars align," but few can achieve great results when perfect conditions are not present or when the momentum shifts away from them. To reach high levels of success, your system must allow you to handle curveballs, while not letting the changes distract you from your ultimate goals. Having a system that is elastic enough to deal with contingencies—situations that can but are not certain to happen—will give you the confidence and ability to keep going when you hit bumps in the road.

Consider how a GPS navigational device works. Although you might miss a turn or have to take a detour, it quickly reroutes you to your destination. The destination does not change because you were rerouted. You might have to go a longer way, and as a result arrive at a later time than originally planned, but you will get there. Elasticity works the same way for your system. Learning to work with Plan Bs allows you to achieve your goals when below optimal situations arise. While developing your personal game plan, you will likely explore several different ways to do something before finding the best one for you. Take good mental notes because some of these different ways may be useful Plan Bs, or backup plans.

I believed in having backup plans, or Plan Bs, for my studies and athletics. For instance, before and during workouts, I would usually talk with my coach about different ways to hit the target times for each run, something that many of my teammates regularly did not do. I figured that the more ways I knew how to reach the same goal, the better I would be at handling circumstances that were not ideal during competitions, such as not properly executing one part of my race or encountering an unexpected move by an opponent. If

I were going to have a shot at winning or doing well, then I could not rely on only best-case scenarios. Similarly, although I preferred to study in certain conditions, sometimes that was not possible, like on road trips. So I adjusted my mind-set and my actions to make the best of the situation. Once I stayed within the rules, how I reached my goal, whether by Plan A or Plan Z, was not as important as that I reached it.

People who consistently succeed do not rely on luck. Besides hard work and sacrifices, they often use systems to gain and maintain their successes and advantages over their competitors. Follow their example. Even though your school provides some basic structures for you and other student-athletes to follow, you should specifically tailor your own personal system or "game plan" toward your individual needs, goals, and potential. If you want to excel in academics, athletics, and other areas of your life, then you need to perfect your personal game plan. Because your time as a student-athlete is relatively short, the sooner you can develop a consistently productive routine, the better.

Remember that the best system for you should maintain or improve your strength areas. Start by building on your strengths, while improving your weaknesses. Again, your system also needs to be *effective, efficient, easily repeatable,* and *elastic.* Spend time perfecting and practicing your game plan so that you can keep improving and stay competitive, no matter what you encounter.

ONE-ON-ONE

- **How do successful people use a personal system to make the most of their time, resources, and potential?**

- **What are some of the benefits of a systematic approach?**

- **Why do you need a good game plan as a student-athlete?**

- **How can you improve your personal system?**

- **What are the "Four Es" of a good personal system?**

7

WATCH YOUR GAME CLOCK

As a track athlete—and particularly a sprinter—I always knew that time mattered. During my collegiate career, I set two NCAA records by fractions of a second, and as a professional athlete, I missed winning my second Olympic medal by thousandths of a second! Unlike me, your success or failure may not be measured in fractions of a second, but you already know the importance of time if you play a sport with time constraints or if you have ever crammed for an exam.

I understood the importance of maximizing every moment in college, even though I often failed to do so. I knew that my eligibility as a student-athlete was limited, so I needed to reach as many goals as I could before my time expired. The same is true for you. From your first day on campus as a student-athlete, your clock is ticking, and you need to know how to deal with dozens of different demands on your time, especially because many of them will be exciting and new to you. You may forget, but your clock is continually counting down, and one day it will reach zero.

Because of NCAA rules, you can and should know the last possible date that you can have collegiate eligibility—this is your "game clock." You can't run out to the meter and put in more quarters to prolong your athletic eligibility. There are no overtimes or replays, and except in rare circumstances, the clock will not stop for any student-athlete. Like fossil fuels, such as coal, petroleum, and natural gas, your collegiate eligibility is nonrenewable. When your time is up, it's up, and you will have to live with whether you made the most of it for the rest of your life.

REALITY CHECK:
As a student-athlete, you do *not* have time on your side. Every day that passes brings you that much closer to the end of your collegiate career.

Unfortunately for many, this reality does not sink in until it is too late. They are like athletes who fail to make the big play before time expires because they did not keep track of the game clock. You don't have to be in that group. Constantly watching your game clock can be a great motivator. The sooner you learn how to make every second count, the more successful you will be before your time as a student-athlete ends. Using your time wisely will help you to accomplish more in every area of your college career and prepare you for your professional future. It often does not seem so, but every moment of every day as a student-athlete is valuable and certainly irreplaceable, even the mundane ones.

When you control your time, you control your success.

YOU ALREADY MANAGE YOUR TIME

Each of us develops a time management system, often subconsciously over a long period, based mainly on our personal values. From our childhood, we start assigning value to activities and spend our time accordingly. We tend to give top priority to what we value most. As my father once told me, you always make time for what you want to do. For instance, when you rush home after training on a Thursday afternoon and carve out time to study *before* getting ready to go to a party, you are managing your time well because you value your schoolwork enough to make it a top priority. On the other hand, if socializing means more to you than your academics, then partying, hanging out, or chatting with friends would be higher priorities and therefore get more quality time than your schoolwork. Most times it is really as simple as giving the most time to what means the most to you. The key to good time management is ensuring that you have the right priorities.

REALITY CHECK:
When your priorities are wrong,
you will manage your time poorly.

Some student-athletes are naturally good at getting everything done properly and on time, while most do only an average job. Even with twenty-four hours at their disposal, a few never seem to have enough hours in the day to do what really is most important. This failure to manage time properly often affects their lives academically, athletically, and personally. The consequences of continually not finishing tasks properly because of poor time management may cause you to feel more stressed and may even jeopardize your eligibility. Here's how I learned the true importance of proper time management in college.

One semester, I decided to take twenty-one credit hours instead of my usual fifteen credit hour course load. This was a crazy idea considering it was also during my season. The extra six credit hours of class time per week plus the schoolwork required for each of those courses significantly affected my whole life. During those first few stressful weeks, I constantly wondered how I was going to hold everything together that semester. I felt overwhelmed by my schoolwork and the pressures to perform on the field. I also slept less than usual and hardly had any "me" time. Then I figured out that during this semester more than any other, I had to manage my time better. I needed to make every moment count by ensuring that my academics and athletics *always* were my top priorities. This meant revamping my entire schedule and changing many habits so I could become more productive and reduce my wasted time. This was not always easy, but I stayed focused on my main goals, and I frequently forced myself to make the necessary sacrifices during the semester to get the job done.

REALITY CHECK:
If you want to do well as a two-sport athlete or when you carry a heavy course load, then you will need to step up your time management, personal organization, and self-discipline.

CONSEQUENCES OF YOUR TIME MANAGEMENT

Proper time management helps you reach more of your goals. Setting aside specific times for each activity will help simplify your life, make you work more efficiently, and help you avoid missing important events or deadlines. Properly prioritizing different commitments in your life sets the groundwork for future success.

Good Time Management

- Lets you use your "best energy," when you feel the most positive, focused, and refreshed, to do a job.
- Allows you to accomplish the most important tasks on your list properly and on time. You give your "best energy" to your top priorities.
- Streamlines your efforts by helping you to discard or replace less productive habits or ideas with better ones. You work smarter, not just harder.
- Helps you to turn current small opportunities into future newer and bigger ones. Finishing smaller tasks properly and on schedule often lays the groundwork for bigger accomplishments.
- Helps you avoid burnout and excessive stress. You will feel more energized and focused because you stay on schedule and hit your deadlines.
- Lets you adapt to unexpected changes. A flexible and efficient schedule allows you to shift some activities around to accomplish what is most important or pressing at that moment without messing up everything else.
- Above all, includes time for adequate rest and downtime.

Poor Time Management

- Results from failing to categorize and prioritize properly which tasks are most important and how long each one should take you to complete.
- Will often lead you to perform at less than your best.

- Makes you vulnerable to failure. You continually scramble to finish your most important tasks right before your time is up.
- Will leave you feeling more drained than you need to be. Regularly feeling stressed means that you are giving your "best energy" to the wrong things.
- Leads to poor compromises between what you want to do and what you need to do.
- Could jeopardize your relationships by causing conflict with others who depend upon you to do things at specific times.

TIPS FOR IMPROVING YOUR TIME MANAGEMENT

Evaluate your present time management—Examining how well you now use your time can help you to determine where you need to adjust your schedule to become more productive. Take a good look at every activity now in your life, including your schoolwork, athletics, and social life. Try not to leave out anything that you regularly do, big or small, especially if it takes significant chunks of your time. Besides noting what these activities are, consider when and for how long you normally do them. Combine and write them down in one place, in a notebook or on your computer. Putting everything together in a comprehensive and chronological format allows you to see systematically and objectively what areas in your present time management are productive or wasteful.

Categorize and prioritize properly—How often have you spent too much or too little time doing something, from watching movies to doing schoolwork to warming up for a competition? We often do things without a clear picture of how much time they usually should take us to finish because we do not categorize and prioritize them properly. Not everything you want to do or need to do has the same importance. Some activities are more important by their nature, such as your schoolwork and athletics; and others, because of their timing, such as rushing to buy a pair of flip-flops for tomorrow's spring break trip before the mall closes. How well you categorize and prioritize in your life makes all the difference in how well you use your time.

Most of your activities will fall under two broad categories: what you need to do—the nonnegotiable and essentials—and what you want to do—the negotiable and nonessentials. We already established that your schoolwork and athletics should be essential activities to you, but how do you categorize your relationships, your involvement in extracurricular organizations, watching certain TV shows, sleep and rest, buying groceries, or doing your laundry? Are those essential or nonessential activities to you?

Besides categorizing your activities, try to prioritize or rank each of them according to their relative level of importance. Here are a few points to consider when doing this: What *must* be done for you to maintain your status as a student-athlete? What has greater long-term potential or payoff? What has the smallest window of opportunity? What is most time sensitive or has to be completed soonest? What is an essential building block for other activities? Answering these questions honestly may cause you to recategorize and reorder your priorities.

The "Importance-Time Matrix" (shown on the next page) is a useful and easy-to-use tool for categorizing and prioritizing your activities. Activities are placed into one of its four quadrants based on their level of importance and the time frame in which they have to be done. For example, studying for a major exam that will be given tomorrow would be considered "Essential-Immediate." However, working on a paper worth only ten percent of your final grade due two months from now could be considered "Essential-Not Immediate." Rushing home to catch a new episode of your favorite TV show may be viewed as "Nonessential-Immediate," while watching a rerun of that same show could be regarded as "Nonessential-Not Immediate." Determining where an activity lies in this matrix can help you to create a more productive time schedule.

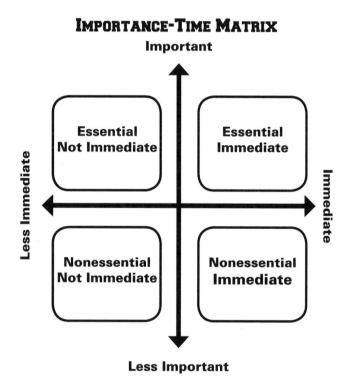

IMPORTANCE-TIME MATRIX

Important

Less Immediate

Immediate

| Essential Not Immediate | Essential Immediate |

| Nonessential Not Immediate | Nonessential Immediate |

Less Important

Remember, the better you can balance what you want to do with what you need to do, the more successful you will be.

Record, update, and review your schedule regularly— Recording your activities makes it easier to look ahead at your full schedule for the day, week, month, semester, or beyond. Seeing in advance what you have to do and when and where tasks have to be done gives you a chance to arrange items according to your priorities and to make better use of your time.

You are probably already skilled at using your cell phones, PDAs, and computers, so put them to work to keep you organized and up to date by using their scheduling functions, such as calendars or to-do lists. Don't forget to sync and back up all your information regularly so that your schedule is complete, accurate, and safe. Of course, you can also use "old-school" tools like time worksheets, bulletin boards, planners, or wall calendars to stay on top of your schedule. These "stone age" methods may not be as fancy or portable as electronic ones, but they often are straightforward to use and reliable.

Try to record everything that you have to do as soon as possible and keep updating your to-do list or schedule as needed. Don't rely only on your memory, especially when changes in date, time, or location are made to important activities. Take time to review your schedule every day so that you can prepare properly for what is coming in the days or weeks ahead, such as term papers, exams, competitions, or appointments. This will help you avoid losing track or confusing dates. Making hard copies of your schedule is a good form of backup and often allows you to do quick reviews and edits to your timetable.

Put first things first—Your personal schedule should always include the most important things that you have to do. Whatever is at the top of your to-do list should be consistent with your core beliefs and your goals of becoming the best student-athlete and person that you can be. Those are the activities in the "Essential" quadrants of your Importance-Time Matrix. As a rule, the best approach is to start with the nonnegotiable activities and work from there to create a schedule that is realistic and productive.

As a student-athlete, your most important resources for creating a good personal schedule are your class syllabuses and your training and competition schedules. These will give you most of the important dates and times for commitments in your studies and sports, from the beginning of the semester. Fortunately, some of this work is already done for you. For instance, you will have predefined times for training and competing, courtesy of your school and coaches. You will also know your class schedule for the semester after you register for classes. Start with these givens and add on from there.

As the semester progresses, coaches and professors tend to add unscheduled practices, assignments, and tests, and you need to know when and where these are taking place so that you can prepare properly. Be flexible enough to deal with such changes. Also be prepared to reassign or cut out less important activities so you can complete more important ones properly or on schedule.

Try to accomplish your most important tasks using your "best energy," when you are freshest and at your best. Give them the prime slots and schedule other activities around them. Tackle the most challenging projects at the best time for you, when you are well rested and before the usual distractions mount, because you will be the most productive. For many, this time is earlier in the day. In other words, if you have important reading or a difficult assignment to do, don't wait until you start getting tired or time is running out to do it because you will likely not do it as well as you could have. Give yourself the best chance to do well at what matters most in the long run.

Your schedule will also include numerous other important appointments, events, or dates not directly related to your academics or athletics. After all, you will want to make time in your schedule to visit with family, socialize with friends, and take care of important tasks such as buying groceries, doing your laundry, or cleaning your room. Again, use the Importance-Time Matrix to help when scheduling these activities.

Don't forget that you need to build in time for sleep too. Adequate rest allows your mind and body to recover properly and gives you more energy, which helps you accomplish more with your time.

Be realistic about using your time—Besides your athletic and academic commitments, many other people and things compete for your time and attention.

REALITY CHECK:
You cannot do well on the field and in the classroom and be involved in everything else you want to do. You have to make choices. If you try to do everything, then chances are you will spread yourself too thin, burn out, and never be as good as you could be at anything.

At some point, you have to draw the line between what you will or won't do and what you can or can't do. You must also sacrifice some activities so that you can give your best in other, more important areas. It can be tough, but learn how and when to say "no" or "later" to yourself and to others about some choices that are not essential to becoming the best student-athlete or person that you can be.

Use practical estimates about how much time you should set aside for each task so you complete each one properly and avoid overscheduling. Base your estimates on how long it normally takes you to do something, not on best-case scenarios. For example, let's say a typical drive from your apartment to campus takes fifteen minutes without traffic but longer in morning rush-hour traffic. It does not make sense to leave your apartment before your morning classes based on the time it takes you to drive to campus with little or no traffic— you will arrive late. Instead, to avoid the hassle of rushing to your morning classes, try leaving twenty or thirty minutes earlier than normal to allow for unusually heavy traffic, accidents, bad weather, and finding parking. Of course, you may need to go to bed a few minutes earlier the night before, but it may be worth not starting your day feeling stressed.

Add even more time to your estimate when tackling new or harder activities. For instance, suppose you have to learn a complex software program for an important course. Give yourself extra time up front to become comfortable with using it. This could save you a lot of time and frustration later when you have to use the software to complete harder assignments. It may also help you to earn a better grade in the course.

When possible, pace yourself by alternating major tasks with easy-to-complete minor ones. Try to avoid overlapping important tasks that require more time or higher concentration. Taking on too much at once or not taking adequate breaks can really throw you off track and cause you to mentally fatigue sooner.

Create a no-procrastination zone— Procrastination means putting off until later what you could or should be doing now. My mother always used to tell me, "Procrastination is a thief of time." She was right. It robs you of achieving your best results, reaching your goals, and realizing your true potential because it puts you in "catch-up" mode rather than in "optimal" mode.

Procrastination often leads to jobs piling up. These in turn can raise your stress levels because of the pressure to get things done in less than ideal circumstances or when time is expiring.

Procrastinating until the deadline might leave you unprepared or unable to finish tasks. You can avoid these issues by handling your business when you are supposed to. Regardless of why you procrastinate, such as being overwhelmed, being forgetful, or lacking interest, you cannot constantly put off tasks and achieve your best or gain a reputation as reliable.

Let's say that you had five weeks to write a term paper, worth thirty percent of your final grade. Unfortunately you procrastinated until the final weekend to work on it. Although your professor warned the class that turning in papers even one minute late would result in an automatic grade reduction, you finished typing yours only an hour before the deadline. This type of procrastination is a recipe for failure. Here's how this scenario can play out:

You hurry to the school's computer lab to print your paper, but all the computers are in use. You hop in your car and rush to the nearest print shop off campus, a trip that takes you fifteen valuable minutes and costs you way too much money.

You print the paper and speed back to campus. Then you waste another five minutes circling the parking lot looking for an empty space before finally giving up and illegally parking in a reserved spot. You know that campus police give out hefty parking tickets or tow violators, but you now have no other option if you want to hand in your paper on time.

Fortunately, your training kicks in. You high-step-it to your professor's office, and you hand in your paper two minutes before the deadline. Although you are drenched in sweat and your heart is about to explode, at least you are safe. You walk away feeling drained and relieved at pulling it off and swear for the nth time that you will "never do that again." Then it hits you! Oh no! You forgot to cite the sources correctly in your paper. Of course to top it off, you'll be $25 poorer because of your parking violation.

Procrastination will get you every time.

Keep to your schedule—Creating a workable personal schedule is key to good time management, but you need to exercise consistent self-discipline for your schedule to be effective in your daily life. Keeping to your schedule is another way of being proactive toward reaching your goals because it puts you in control of your time. It often requires making sacrifices and monitoring your time so that your downtime, when you rest and recharge, does not unintentionally become wasted time, when you do nothing productive or positive.

REALITY CHECK:
If you are not careful with your time, you can easily lose track of it and find yourself way off schedule.

Most cell phones have clock, alarm, and alert functions that can help you to stay on time. However, some circumstances may make them inappropriate to use, such as during an exam or at competitions. Using a wristwatch may help you to avoid those problems, and it is another great way to become more time conscious. Successful people often use wristwatches because they know that proper time management contributes much to their achievements. My wristwatch was probably my "best friend" in college. I always used it during my warm-ups, exams, and study sessions. Similarly, you can use your watch to stay on schedule when doing schoolwork or playing sports. For example, you can set the alarm function on your watch to avoid oversleeping, particularly when you plan to take a short nap before studying or competing, and to arrive on schedule for appointments. The more time conscious you become, the more valuable your time becomes.

Of course, no matter what tool you use to assist you, the

best time management is still always in your head. You decide every day how to manage your time and whether you will keep to your schedule. The good news is that being organized and finishing tasks properly and on schedule can give you extra time for your social life, personal interests, or more rest.

NO TIME LIKE NOW

I was methodical about using my schedule to accomplish my top priorities—my studies and athletics—and other activities that were important to me, such as being involved in my local church or doing some type of community work. That often meant sacrificing or limiting other activities, depending on how much free time I had or what else I needed to do.

Ironically, although most of my days were busy, I hardly felt overwhelmed or stressed. This was because I tried to stay on top of important matters from the start instead of procrastinating and letting them pile up. For example, I used my syllabuses to map out what I needed to do in my courses days or weeks in advance, especially for important exams or term papers. I also used my competition schedule to get physically and mentally ready weeks before specific competitions, particularly championships or key match-ups against top rivals. Although I could work well under pressure, I still tried to avoid putting my mind and body under any more stress than necessary. I learned that habitual cramming or rushing to get ready was less effective than progressively preparing well in advance.

I wish that I had rested more while in college. I usually went to bed around 1 a.m. every day. This pattern probably had much to do with the fact that I grew up in a household where everyone regularly went to sleep after 11 p.m. Although I worked better at nights than during the daytime, constantly going to sleep late and waking up early for classes took its toll on me. Some days, my focus in class and my energy during training were so low that I was barely functional. Of course, this set me up to fall behind in my classes or to sustain an injury—not smart moves on my part.

Also, despite constantly using my wristwatch, I was usually late or just on time for most appointments and functions. I am not sure why I struggled with punctuality apart from my exams and competitions. Perhaps it was because I usually underestimated how long it should take me to get ready or to get to where I needed to be. Or maybe it was my tendency to be indecisive or do unnecessary things right before I headed out. Regardless of the reasons, sometimes my lateness frustrated others who waited or relied on me to be somewhere or to do something at set times. On some occasions my lateness led to arguments with others or having to postpone or cancel certain activities. You can do yourself a big favor by resting properly and being reliably punctual.

Apply all your skills and talents to maximize your relatively short time as a student-athlete. Remember, once you control your time, you control your success. Learning to categorize and prioritize tasks and activities properly is critical. A workable personal schedule will help you to organize your essential and nonessential activities effectively and may even give you more time for other personal interests. Since you cannot do everything, at some point you must determine what you can and cannot do. Allocate your time realistically among your activities and put first things first. Effective time management is one of the most important life skills you can develop and being a student-athlete gives you the perfect chance to perfect it. Remember to make big plans for your future and always watch your game clock!

ONE-ON-ONE

- How aware are you of your "game clock" every day as a student-athlete? Do you know your last possible date of eligibility?

- What are three consequences of good time management and of poor time management?

- How are unrealistic time estimations, not putting first things first, procrastinating, or wasting time affecting your success?

- What is the Importance-Time Matrix and how can it help you to improve your time management?

- What should you do when you are not able to do everything that you need or want to do?

STAY "INBOUNDS" WHEN YOU'RE OFF THE FIELD

Several years ago, I consulted a world-renowned nutritionist about designing a dietary supplement program for me. At the time, my poor eating and sleeping habits had finally caught up with me. My immune system had become very weak, which severely limited my ability to train properly. Surprisingly his main interest was not on my diet but on my lifestyle. He recommended a supplement program but told me that my biggest gains would come from improving my lifestyle. Even though I had been a world-ranked athlete in my sport for many years, I still underestimated the important relationship between lifestyle and performance.

Your lifestyle is your way of life or how you live. Although past and present circumstances influence your lifestyle, your choices usually mirror your personal values and character. For example, when your values are out of whack, then you will likely live without consistent balance, focus, and self-control. These can lead to poor decision making, subpar results, and not being able to take full advantage of opportunities. In contrast, if your values are properly aligned, then you are likely to live positively with moderation, purpose, and discipline. These traits usually lead to making good decisions, achieving your potential, and enjoying lasting personal fulfillment. Of course, it is not really that straightforward because we all have some "good" and some "bad" values and traits that affect how we live each day. However, it is important to remember that your lifestyle affects your performance as a student-athlete.

In many ways, this entire book is about helping you to create a lifestyle that allows you to succeed as a student-athlete and in life. This chapter alone could easily be a book. Instead I will highlight only a few key lifestyle issues and offer some suggestions about ways to improve your lifestyle so you can improve your performance.

LOWER YOUR STRESS

Everyone lives with some stress. It comes from various sources and affects people differently. It also comes in different intensities and lasts for different durations. Some stress is avoidable and controllable, but not all stress is bad. Sometimes stress can be a catalyst for growth, improvement, or change. How much stress you have and how you handle it can affect you emotionally, physically, mentally, and spiritually. Eventually, if not dealt with properly, high stress levels, like trouble, can compound, wear you down, and stop you from performing at your best.

Because of the pressures to do well in the classroom and on the field, you will likely feel stressed at different times throughout the semester and season—this is normal. For instance, stress usually increases when you have important exams and competitions, poor grades, a subpar season, or injuries.

Ideally, the best way to handle stress is to stop it from building up in any area by simplifying your life. Of course, this is easier said than done. Although you cannot avoid stress entirely, you can manage and reduce it.

Here are some useful "stress busters":

- Properly categorize and prioritize tasks such as essential versus nonessential and immediate versus not immediate deadlines.
- Know what you need to do, and plan to do it properly and on time the first time.
- Know your limits and do not regularly take on more than you can handle. Limit your commitments not directly related to being a student-athlete and learn the art of saying "no" or "later."
- Always do the right thing and make choices that are best for you in the long run.
- Get help from the right people at the right time, preferably before your back is against the wall.

Remember, controlling and lowering your stress improves your likelihood of doing well because you will have greater focus and energy to do what you need to do.

CONTROL YOUR SOCIAL LIFE BEFORE IT RULES YOU

Like most college students, your social life plays a big part in your college experience. It can influence your self-image, goals, values, attitudes, habits, choices, and actions. Your social life can be a lot of fun and even provide some relief from stress, but if you are not careful it could also "rule" you—this is not a good thing. Many student-athletes struggle to find the right balance for a number of common social issues, including sex, partying, extracurricular organizations, their environments, and their relationships. Let's take a closer look at some of these issues.

Sex is a titillating and touchy topic for most student-athletes—actually, for many people—and it could easily be a chapter or book itself. It is a complex and personal matter, which can affect you physically, emotionally, spiritually, and even legally. Issues such as your sexual preference, whether heterosexual, gay, or bisexual; your sexual habits, including having one or more sexual partners at a time; and how you express your individual sexuality, such as your appearance, conversations, or conduct, can influence what circumstances you face as well as how others view you and your self-worth. College often provides many opportunities to explore and express your sexuality with other young people driven by curiosity, passion, and hormones, but you need to be careful.

Engaging in sexual activities when you are not ready or feel pressured can lead to regrets later. Also, never force anyone to participate in sexual activities without first getting their clear consent. Even with the other person's consent, there are times that you should think carefully before you proceed to have sex, such as when you or the other person is inebriated, underage, or cheating. Such cases can become very complicated, legally and otherwise, when emotions, hormones, or the "high" wear off.

Always use proper protection if you have sex, regardless of who your partner is or what he or she claims. This can reduce your risk of unplanned pregnancies and contracting or spreading sexually transmitted diseases (STDs) such as HIV, gonorrhea, chlamydia, or herpes. Bear in mind that apart from abstinence, there is no 100 percent guarantee that preventative measures will work—they sometimes fail.

Unfortunately, I had some female friends whose lives were changed forever because of unplanned pregnancies. As young adults barely past their teens, they had to face the incredibly tough decision about whether to have an abortion or to potentially end their college careers by letting their pregnancies go full-term. I also saw how "baby mama" and "baby daddy" drama emotionally and financially stressed some student-athletes. Of course, I also witnessed other student-athletes become distracted and waste lots of energy and money being "players," living double or triple lives with their various sexual partners.

Get tested regularly if you are sexually active, especially if you have more than one sexual partner or if your sexual partner has slept with someone else. Most student health centers have many resources about sexually related matters, so visit your campus center if you want to get tested or have any questions or concerns. Also, don't forget that in college some people like to gossip and spread your business, so be mindful with whom you talk and about what you say, especially with highly personal issues.

Although it might seem obvious, don't forget that sex and love are *not* the same. So if you are seeking love and think that having sex is the solution, prepare for disappointment and more problems. Instead, you may benefit from building your self-esteem in other ways first. Be smart about your sexual choices and partners. I know it is not always easy to do when your emotions and hormones are high, but stop for a second to consider the consequences of having sex with someone before you proceed. "Just do it" is a great slogan for many things, but not necessarily when it comes to having sex while you're in college.

REALITY CHECK:
One sexual encounter can change your life and those of others forever, so be careful.

Partying can be a great way to enjoy yourself, release stress, and socialize. Parties on and off campus are popular at most schools and can be a lot of fun, but be smart about where and when you party. Try to avoid partying at places prone to illegal activities and unnecessary drama. You may be better off skipping a party where you are tempted to make choices that are not in your best interest, such as getting drunk or high, or engaging in conflict with others for personal reasons or because of your school affiliation.

Some people at parties may target you as a student-athlete for various reasons, such as envy, a chance for them to become more popular because of their association with you, or even because of your earning potential if you have a legitimate chance at becoming a professional athlete. These types of situations can become troublesome for you, so pay attention to those around you when you party. Be mindful of potential NCAA violations, such as accepting VIP "hookups" because you are a student-athlete. Don't forget that as a student-athlete you will likely be remembered by others, especially if you are in the wrong place at the wrong time or doing the wrong thing.

REALITY CHECK:
No party is worth jeopardizing your personal safety and reputation.

A few years ago, there was a highly publicized incident involving several male student-athletes at a prominent school, falsely accused of raping a female exotic dancer who was providing "entertainment" for a team party. Because of the scandal, the president of their school canceled the remainder of the team's season that year and their coach resigned under pressure. The incident also stirred great local and national debate, touching on many issues including racism, the actions of the prosecutor (who later resigned for unethical conduct), the role of media reporting on the incident, and, of course, the behavior of student-athletes in general. Although all charges against the players were dropped—and rightfully so— their lives and the lives of many others were changed forever because of that party.

Partying hard and regularly can use lots of energy. Keep this in mind when you have important schoolwork, hard training, or major competitions, so you don't leave your best performance on the dance floor. Find the proper balance so that you will be ready to perform at your best when it matters most.

Some years ago, a good friend and I reminisced about our own college days. He confessed that when he first came to college, his main mission was to party and to sleep with as many women as possible. If there was a party, he was there, and he seldom turned down an opportunity for sex. Once, after a long night of doing both, he woke up late the following afternoon, only to find that his companion for the night was no longer there. He had no clue when she had left because he was asleep, worn out from the night before.

When he finally called her, he soon realized that while he had just wasted most of his day trying to recover, she had already been studying for hours in preparation for final exams. He said that conversation was a real wakeup call for him. Apparently, he was on the verge of flunking out of school because his social life was out of control. After rearranging his priorities to put his social life in check, his life became more balanced and his schoolwork vastly improved. (He is now a doctor with a successful practice.)

Becoming involved in *extracurricular organizations* can broaden your college experience. It can provide you a chance to expand your network, pursue your personal interests, and give back to your community. Such organizations may range from religious, like fellowship groups, to social, like sororities and fraternities, to political, like student government. Always check with your coaching staff first to see if joining an organization is allowed. Be mindful of how much time you devote to your organization's events and activities. Stay focused on your priorities as a student-athlete, especially if you receive financial aid.

One of my friends decided to join a sorority during her senior year, probably so she could enjoy the benefits of membership in that national organization after graduation. As happens to many others who "pledge," the initiation disrupted her life. While "on line," she often came to practice fatigued and unfocused because she had stayed up late the previous night trying to balance her usual demands as a student-athlete with the constant activities from her "big sisters" before she "crossed over." I doubt that she told her coach before she pledged. He probably would have stopped her had he understood the real reason her athletic performances that season were so poor. Joining the sorority was not her problem, but misplacing her priorities was. Her main loyalty should have been to her school, which paid for her to be there, and to her team, rather than to her sorority sisters.

Your regular *environment*—living area, workspace, and "hangouts" —plays a significant role in how well you perform. If your surroundings are negative, dirty, and disorganized, then you will likely feel less productive and focused. In contrast, a positive, clean, and neatly structured environment often allows you to work with greater clarity and efficiency. For instance, you are likely to study better when your notes are organized and together than when you have to look for them because they are scattered or have been misplaced. When your setting is positive and organized, your choices and actions tend to follow suit.

Almost every year, stories about student-athletes being involved in some illegal activities make national news.

REALITY CHECK:
Wearing your school's colors does not put you above the law or protect you from the consequences of your actions. Under no circumstances should you be involved in selling, using, or possessing illegal drugs, or in any other illegal activity, like physical or sexual assaults, stealing, gambling, or possessing illegal weapons.

Even if you come from a tough background where violence and crime are part of everyday life, you are still responsible for your choices and actions. Protect your opportunities, freedom, and future by making the right choice to stay far from trouble. You may lose some "friends" or "respect" from those caught up in that lifestyle, but you will be better off in the long run. Your regular environment plays a significant role in being able to think clearly and make the right choices for your life.

I once had a friend who seemed to have the gangster movie *Carlito's Way* on permanent repeat—it was always showing whenever I visited him. Not surprisingly, he was constantly in trouble, and I later discovered that he usually kept an illegal gun stashed in his car "just in case." I don't think that he appreciated how much of an impact his overexposure to music, movies, and conversations saturated with profanity, crime, and violence had on his psyche and actions. It was hard from him to stay positive every day on and away from the field, with that constant stream of negativity and very little positive, uplifting, or inspiring input to balance it out. Sadly, his college career ended way too soon after he was arrested for committing a crime.

Although my friend's case was extreme, many people underestimate how much their regular environment affects their lives, including their studies, athletics, and life choices. Because negativity is generally so prevalent in our society, you often have to make an extra effort to create a positive balance. Without this balance you may unintentionally find yourself drifting in the wrong direction, around the wrong people, doing the wrong things, or in the wrong circumstances. Monitor and control your environment and feed yourself good "brain food."

Relationships are among the most important aspects of life, and you will have many types of them during college. Most will be the result of timing, location, need, or common interests. Over time, you will form new relationships and become closer to some people, while other relationships will end or become less close. Relationships are dynamic and can sometimes be challenging because they involve people, and all people change, including you. All relationships require some work, mainly patience, respect, and understanding.

How well you manage your relationships tends to impact how well you perform academically and on the field. In college, *romantic relationships* are often intense and volatile. Amazingly, the same person who makes you feel that you can fly can also make you feel terrible. Romantic relationships can affect your self-esteem, self-confidence, focus, and productivity. They can also affect your sleep and diet. In fact, if you are not careful, they can dominate your life. I learned this the hard way.

My world almost instantly turned upside down after I was blindsided by a "Dear John" (actually, "Dear Oba") letter, notifying me that I had been "dumped." The timing of that news could not have been worse because I was already dealing with a lot of other stuff in my life. Unfortunately, at the time I did not know how to stop systemic hemorrhaging—allowing something "bad" in one area to affect my whole life. I hate to admit this, but I felt depressed for about a year after reading that letter. I struggled to stay focused academically and athletically (that's an understatement), and my self-esteem and motivation reached all-time lows. Fortunately, I still did well because I had practiced many of the "secrets" in this book, like how to study and train effectively, for so long that they were almost automatic even when I was emotionally absent or mostly unmotivated.

Besides my personal experiences, I have seen romantic relationships significantly influence people's personalities, lifestyles, careers, finances, and even their other relationships—for better or worse. Try to keep these relationships healthy, nonabusive, and mutually beneficial so that you can grow positively through them without losing sight of what is most important as a student-athlete.

REALITY CHECK:
About half of the marriages today end in divorce and the breakup rate in college is probably higher. Bear this in mind before you sacrifice what you should be doing every day as a student-athlete for a romantic relationship.

Relationships with *family members* can also have an effect on you in several ways, including emotionally and even financially. Sometimes your relationship with them can change significantly based on how much you or they change while you are at college. For instance, your experiences with people from different backgrounds may cause you to rethink your own upbringing or question your family's value system. Or certain ideas that you encounter during your courses may reshape your understanding or convictions on topics from religion to education and politics—views that may not be openly welcomed at your home. Of course, you will likely also go through the usual transition of exerting yourself so that you can be accepted as an "adult" by family members. Hopefully, you can do this without too much conflict or being viewed—rightfully or not—as disrespectful or unappreciative.

As I mentioned several times, the loving support of my family was instrumental to my success as a student-athlete. Although I always tried to be respectful toward my parents, there were some epic and heated exchanges between my father and me while I was in college. Most of these occurred because we did not always see eye to eye on certain things related to my athletic career, my changing views on issues, and what he thought I should do versus what I wanted to do. I recall my poor mother trying to mediate one such conversation that happened about three minutes after they picked me up from the airport for the Christmas holidays. Within ten minutes, it was so intense that I told my father to turn around and drop me off at the airport so that I could return to school. My mother finally calmed us down before my father could oblige my request.

I know that various other issues, like respecting your parents' rules about curfew or what you can do "under their roof" can cause tension. However, it is usually best if you try to enjoy, or at least make the most of, your interactions with family so that you have less tension. This may mean obeying some rules while you are around them during holidays, avoiding certain hot topics, or accepting them for who they are or despite what they believe, even if you think or feel differently. Regardless of what you learn or experience in college, don't forget who raised you or about the sacrifices they made for you to enjoy the privileges you now receive.

Your relationships with your *coaches and teammates* will affect how well you train and compete. Earlier I mentioned the importance of developing your relationships with your coaches, but you should also make an effort to develop your relationships with your teammates. This is not always easy because you may not naturally jell with everyone on your team. In fact, there may be some friction or rivalries between you and some of your teammates—I know this firsthand. I also know the frustration of being on "teams" when we all did not have the same goals or effort, and when personal issues interfered with us getting the job done. You don't need to be best buddies with your teammates, but you need to learn to have civil and functional relationships with them, particularly during training and competitions. Try your best to reduce whatever tension is among you. Remember, it is difficult to do well in team sports when there is infighting and when good team chemistry is lacking.

Your *roommates* at school and on the road matter. Your relationships with them affect much of your college experience because you have to deal with them almost every day. Their habits, attitudes, and personalities can have a significant impact on your quality of life. Their presence can also influence your sleeping and studying habits, productivity, personal safety, wallet, behavior, and focus. I know that your coaches or school may preassign certain roommates, but if possible, try to room with someone who shares compatible values and a similar lifestyle. Doing this from the start may save you much tension, frustration, and even money.

Bear in mind that a good friend does not always make a good roommate because you may have different living habits or they may do things that you can tolerate in the short term but not for an entire semester or school year. For example, you may discover important differences in your tidiness, organization, sleeping habits, handling of financial obligations, visitor rules, attitudes toward academics, athletic and personal responsibilities, and respect for others and their property. Hanging out and partying with someone is not the same as rooming with them.

REALITY CHECK:
Constant friction between you
and your roommates is exactly what you
don't need in order to do well.

I once allowed a good friend to room with me for a few weeks after the lease on his apartment had expired. One day, he discovered that I stored my calling card, which I used to make international calls back home, in a certain drawer. When he asked for permission to use it to call his girlfriend, I told him no because my parents paid the bill—he and I were cool, but he wasn't family.

Later that summer, after returning home for the holidays, I received a thick envelope from the calling card company. I instantly knew something was not right. At the end of the seventeen-page phone bill, I saw a total for over $1,300. Most of those charges were from calls to my friend's girlfriend's house. I could not believe that he had betrayed my trust and not simply used, but abused, my calling card after I clearly told him not to use it. My father wanted to take some legal action against my three-week "roommate," but I protected my friend. Although we saw each other several times afterward, it took over five years for my friend to step up and apologize to me for stealing my calling card number. As I said, be careful when choosing your roommates.

Be mindful of the company you regularly keep—*"friends and associates."* Not only can being around others affect your reputation, it can also influence your choices and the circumstances you find yourself facing, for better or worse. These relationships should cause you to advance and grow, not pull you down. Think about the people who are frequently in your life now and decide if, for your own best interest, you may have to change how much contact you have with some of them. You will benefit greatly when you stick around positive, ambitious, and disciplined people who challenge themselves and you to become better.

TAKE CARE OF YOUR BODY

Your body is perhaps your biggest asset; how you treat it affects you in several ways, good or bad. Conventional wisdom about nutrition usually goes like this: garbage in, garbage out (GIGO). You cannot put low-grade fuel into your body and expect high-grade results. For instance, if you give most luxury cars requiring premium gas regular gas, they will still work, but they will eventually underperform. They might even suffer engine damage because they are not getting the right fuel to work as designed, let alone perform at their best. Similarly, as a student-athlete, your body requires premium "gas" or fuel so it can function at its best, especially because it is constantly being pushed. Although you can survive or even do well eating poorly, you won't achieve your best possible performance.

REALITY CHECK:
Your diet significantly impacts
both your studies and your athletics.

Even so, many champion athletes still have terrible diets. In fact, based on personal experiences and observations, I would estimate that most student-athletes do not have well-balanced diets. Poor diets and eating habits, like eating junk food, are so common because of cost, convenience, and poor education about proper nutrition.

When I was in high school, my parents tried in vain to get me to eat well by including more vegetables and fruits in my diet. Unfortunately, my poor eating habits continued in college. For example, when I was a freshman at my first NCAA Indoor Championships, my coach told me that I needed to "eat something" between my races. I had no clue of what to eat and I did not ask him for suggestions because I never ate during competitions. Later that day, while I was between events, I passed a vending machine in the stadium and remembered his instructions to me. Two dollar bills less, and a Snickers candy bar and a can of Sprite were my "meal" for the day—definitely not the food of champions.

Because I saw countless other student-athletes do well with poor diets, I cannot say you won't excel without a well-balanced diet. I strongly believe that, with a better diet, I could have accomplished more. Science has shown there are several benefits to a well-balanced diet, including greater alertness, focus, and energy, and a more robust immune system to fight illness. A proper diet also reduces your risk of injury and allows you to work longer and harder.

How much and when you eat can significantly shape your body composition, particularly your body weight and your body mass index (BMI). Body composition affects athletic performance, especially in weight-sensitive sports like wrestling and gymnastics. It may also affect how you feel physically, such as heavy or sluggish, and otherwise, including how you feel about your appearance. If you are new to college, beware of the infamous "Freshman 15," so-called because many new student-athletes gain about fifteen pounds at the start of their college life. This occurs for several reasons, including a more intensive weight program, eating the wrong foods, and eating at the wrong times. Beware of those late-night "munchies," like candy and other unhealthy snacks, especially when you are studying.

If you need help making an affordable and practical diet, then visit with your trainer or a school-approved dietician or nutritionist. They likely have useful meal ideas to fit your nutritional needs and budget. Some schools also provide training tables for their student-athletes with healthy meal plan options. Whether or not this choice is available to you, make good choices about your diet and eating habits. Try to eat the right foods, at the right time, and in the right amounts. Also, always stay properly hydrated with water or electrolyte drinks with low sugar content, not sodas, particularly when you have to study, train, or compete hard. Plan ahead for meals instead of always eating whatever happens to be cheapest or easiest at the time.

Although many do not talk openly about it, thousands of student-athletes, male and female, suffer from eating disorders, mainly anorexia and bulimia. This hypersensitivity to weight affects how, when, and what someone eats in an unhealthy and compulsive way. Eating disorders are classified under mental health illnesses because they are often symptomatic of deeper issues. Not only can they disrupt your academic and athletic career, they may also cause serious health problems and, in rare cases, can even lead to death.

If you or someone you know displays behavior suggesting an eating disorder, do something about it soon. Fortunately, many resources exist to educate and help those struggling or wishing to learn more about combating these illnesses, including organizations like the National Eating Disorders Association (NEDA) and the National Institute of Mental Health (NIMH). There is no need for you to continue suffering when help is readily available. The sooner you reach out and get help, the sooner you can be on the road to recovery.

Finally, remember that your current diet not only affects you now but also will affect your future health and quality of life.

BE CAREFUL WITH ALCOHOL AND DRUGS

Few student-athletes finish college without using alcohol or drugs because they are available at many college parties, social events, and local nightclubs. Although drinking or doing drugs, as regular students often do, may be statistically normal in college, student-athletes must follow certain rules governing the use of such substances. The NCAA and likely your school have drug and alcohol policies that you should know and follow. These include testing programs with serious consequences for violators.

In the US, alcohol is by far the most accessible and widely used "drug." It falls under federal government regulation because it is dangerous when abused. Each state's drinking age and consumption laws vary—be aware of what they are if you plan to drink at school or on the road. The easy access to alcohol and the social acceptance of drinking probably explain why many student-athletes drink at some time during the school year.

Most drugs that student-athletes abuse are either controlled substances requiring a doctor's prescription, like painkillers and sleeping pills, or those altogether illegal to use or possess. Some people mistakenly underestimate the perils of abusing prescription and over-the-counter medications because they are not "hardcore" drugs. However, abusing these and "street" or "recreational" drugs, such as marijuana, ecstasy, heroin, and cocaine, is dangerous. Hundreds of studies and personal stories document the hazards to your well-being from abusing these kinds of drugs. The risks increase exponentially for street drugs because the government does not regulate their manufacturers and suppliers. There are no standard controls over ingredients, some of which may be lethally potent. In other words, regardless of the source, you never know exactly what is inside those drugs. Abusing these drugs puts your success and career as a student-athlete at risk, and perhaps your life too.

The side effects of abusing alcohol and illegal drugs vary by individual. Common side effects include disorientation, hallucinations, sluggishness, depression, hyperactivity, and aggression, which may lead to verbal or physical altercations. You can lose control of your bodily functions and for example, involuntarily vomit or defecate on yourself. You may also suffer reduced motor skills, which can cause you to become unbalanced, clumsy, and even impair your ability to drive. Dehydration is another common side effect, which could directly affect how well you perform on the field.

Most importantly, the poor decisions you make in a diminished capacity, besides being potentially embarrassing, can have serious consequences. When you are not sober, you are more likely to say or do something that compromises your personal safety, eligibility, status with your school or team, relationships, reputation, freedom, and, in extreme cases, even your life or the lives of others. Although getting drunk or high may seem like a good idea at the time, doing so may cause you far-reaching legal, emotional, and personal troubles, especially in today's culture where people immediately upload videos or pictures taken on digital cameras and cell phones to the Internet.

In college, I rarely drank alcohol besides occasional sips of wine and I avoided doing drugs altogether. I saw firsthand how alcohol robbed a family member of his health and many opportunities, and strained his closest relationships. I also had severe asthma from the age of three, so smoking anything was unattractive and impractical to me.

Even with my reasons and resolve against drinking, during my freshman year I still felt pressure to drink to gain my teammates' acceptance. No one ever tried to force a beer into my hand—being underage probably helped me—but sometimes I felt left out because of my choice not to drink. I recall one night, while a few of us from my team were tailgating before a home football game, that one of the seniors approached me with a brown paper bag. I was surprised because I knew that, like me, he was not a drinker. Before I could launch into my well-rehearsed speech about why I don't drink, he rolled down the paper bag and pointed to the fine print at the bottom of the bottle's label. After a few seconds of reading, the broadest smile crossed my face—I had finally hit the "jackpot." That night, he introduced me to his (our) little secret—O'Doul's nonalcoholic beer! Actually, I did not like how it tasted, but I did like that I could finally "drink beer" like everyone else. As dumb as it seems, drinking beer, even the nonalcoholic type, made me feel socially much more at ease and accepted around my older teammates. Looking back, I don't think that it made much difference to any of them because they knew that I still was not drinking the "real stuff." I know that similar pressures are the main reason many drink, do drugs, smoke cigarettes, or chew tobacco.

Your age, abilities, and accomplishments do not make you immune from the effects of drug and alcohol abuse, which ruin many lives, including those of celebrities and famous athletes. Perhaps this is best illustrated in the unfortunate story of former All-American basketball player Len Bias. Within forty-eight hours of being the number 2 overall pick in the 1986 NBA Draft by the Boston Celtics, he died from a drug overdose. It shocked everyone that an athlete in prime physical shape, with a world of opportunities ahead, could have died so young and so tragically. Investigations later revealed that he and some of his teammates had been "recreational" users of drugs for some time before his death.

Closer to home, I experienced the terrible loss of a friend and teammate because of drunken driving. I also had some friends who unintentionally went from casual users of drugs or alcohol, mainly at parties or on the weekends, to having serious substance abuse issues. For instance, one friend drank and "dipped" chewing tobacco so much that he could hardly finish his events at competitions, and by his early 20s he was admitted to the hospital with serious health problems related to abusing those substances. Another friend, at a top-ranked college in his sport, went from being a potential NCAA champion to losing his financial aid and dropping out of school within two years because he developed a drinking problem in college. Unfortunately I can go on. Another good friend lost his chance of potentially earning millions as a professional athlete because he violated his sport's substance abuse policy by smoking weed. Talk about an expensive "joint!"

Sadly, seeing or hearing about stories like these affect many people for only a short time before they relapse into carefree and dangerous habits. Most people say, "That won't happen to me." How many of these unfortunate victims thought the same thing before tragedy struck them? The reality is that it can happen to *you*, especially if you take chances with your well-being by abusing drugs and alcohol or being around others while they do.

If you or someone you know struggles with alcohol or drug problems, try to get help before it is too late. The longer you wait, the worse it can become, and the more you can lose. Although the first steps, such as admitting your problem and being open to help from others, may be tough, these actions may save your relationships, your opportunities, and even your life. Thankfully, the NCAA, and probably your school, has resources to help restore you to wellness in this area. However, you need to do it for yourself.

Finally, let's get real for a minute. Understandably, the NCAA and your school prefer that you don't drink alcohol or use drugs, but regardless of the dangers, you may still choose to do either or both. I strongly recommend that you don't mess with drugs, but drinking responsibly is an option. Drinking responsibly includes no underage drinking, knowing and staying inside your alcohol tolerance, and ensuring that you have safeguards in place to protect you, such as drinking in a safe environment or having a designated driver. Remember, no one plans to jeopardize their future, but a temporary lapse in judgment can be a life-changer for you and others. The next time you are considering drinking or taking drugs, soberly ask yourself: "Is it really worth the risk?"

SUPPLEMENTS MAYBE, PERFORMANCE-ENHANCING DRUGS (PEDS) NEVER

Sports nutrition—including dietary and nutritional supplements—is a multibillion-dollar industry in the US. Many supplements allow athletes to train and compete with more intensity and aid in recovery. Surprisingly, since 1996, the Food and Drug Administration (FDA) has exercised minimal regulation of supplements. Most companies self-regulate and are responsible for the quality control of their products. Unfortunately, not all companies use the highest quality ingredients or methods to prevent contamination. This can be worrisome if you use supplements because, according to the NCAA drug and alcohol policy, as a student-athlete, you are responsible for *whatever* you consume. Several athletes have innocently used a legal but tainted supplement and failed drug tests.

Be careful about what supplements you take. Do not let advertisements, a salesperson at a health store, teammates, or someone at a local gym persuade you to take *anything*. Their intentions may be good, but they may unintentionally recommend supplements on the NCAA's banned substances list. Check with the person at your school responsible for drug-testing and educating student-athletes about what substances and products are safe to use *before* you try or buy *any* of them. Remember, although you may later be able to prove your innocence, the damage done to your career, reputation, wallet, and team could be significant.

In recent years, many scandals about performance-enhancing drugs (PEDs) have caused great debate among coaches, athletes, fans, and those in the media about their place in sports. In reality, PEDs, mainly anabolic steroids and stimulants, have secretly been a part of many amateur and professional sports for a long time because they can help athletes to train and compete harder and gain an edge over competitors.

The NCAA and most other sports organizations ban the use of PEDs, not only because they can give you an artificial advantage over opponents but also because they can present serious health risks. These health risks arise when PEDs are taken without proper medical supervision, in certain combinations ("stacked"), and over a long time. Some common side effects of using PEDs include high blood pressure, harmful cholesterol levels, acne, heart disease, temporary infertility, and reduced sexual function. Users may also experience mood swings ranging from aggression and violence to depression. Also, because of the close relation of anabolic steroids to testosterone, females using PEDs may undergo changes such as increased body hair, deepening of their voices, and changes in their sex organs and menstrual cycles.

Despite the temptation to use PEDs for their physiological benefits in sports, using them is cheating. If you fail a drug test or you are caught violating the NCAA drug and alcohol policy, you can be temporarily banned from competing in the NCAA or permanently lose your eligibility. You may also do irreparable damage to yourself, your teammates, and your school. Be educated and careful about whatever you take. Come to training and competitions with a good work ethic rather than trying to find the easy way to the top or looking for a "magic" pill or injection to help you improve your game. Take pride in your performances—win or lose—and do not cheat yourself or others.

BE SMART WITH YOUR MONEY

Money is a limited resource for most college students, so how you manage it matters. Budgeting wisely based on when and how much money you normally get usually helps you to take care of yourself and your financial debts properly between your "paydays." Unfortunately because there are thousands of products and services—essential and nonessential—always competing for every dollar in your pocket, smart budgeting is not always easy, but it is doable.

REALITY CHECK:
You will usually mismanage your money when you lack a good financial plan or the discipline to stick to one.

Six Easy Money Management Tips

- Create a personal budget, and always monitor your spending.
- Take care of your most important expenses first.
- Reduce unnecessary or wasteful spending.
- Pay down your outstanding debt.
- Try to save for a "rainy day" or for future purchases.
- Don't buy what you can't now afford.

Beware of the credit card trap—Credit card companies often do promotions on or around college campuses to get students to sign up for their products and services. These offers can be attractive at first—after all, what's cooler than spending money that you don't have?—but the interest rates and penalties in the fine print can quickly put you in great debt if you're late with your payments. As tempting as it may seem to get a credit card, don't sign up for one without first getting your parents' approval.

Be very careful with using credit cards because the debts you accrue during college can often affect your credit report long after graduation. Your credit history usually determines whether you can get loans to buy the home, car, or other items you may later want and the interest rate at which you can get those loans. Countless college students have gotten caught in the trap of maxing out multiple credit cards, only to discover that they had unintentionally trashed their credit with nothing of worth to show for it.

REALITY CHECK:
Credit card companies are not
your friends; they want to rope you in at
a young age so that you wind up paying
on the credit cards for the
rest of your life.

Poor money management can often lead to financial troubles, which can become distracting and stressful and may affect your well-being and how you perform. These troubles may also tempt you to make choices that worsen your circumstances, such as doing illegal or compromising activities for money or neglecting essential purchases like your groceries and your utilities. Be smart with your money and realize that you simply can't afford to purchase everything that you want to right now.

STAY OUT OF "PERSONAL-FOUL" TROUBLE

Your lifestyle either supports or undermines your hard work, talents, and opportunities. Pay attention to it. Stress usually increases when you face important tests and competitions, have low grades or subpar results on the field, or suffer injuries. You can reduce stress by simplifying your life, knowing and doing what you need to do, and not regularly taking on more than you can handle.

Pay special attention to common problem areas for student-athletes, such as your sex life, partying, involvement in extracurricular organizations, your environment, and your relationships. Thoroughly enjoy your social life, but don't let it rule you. Learning to balance your social life with the many other commitments that demand your time and energy allows you to experience college at its fullest. Also, budget and use your money wisely so that you can take care of yourself and your bills and avoid financial troubles.

Your body is your biggest asset as a student-athlete. How you maintain your fitness on all levels—physical, mental, emotional, and spiritual—greatly affects your well-being. In other words, your body and mind won't perform at their best if you regularly mistreat them by, for example, a poor diet, inadequate rest and recovery, or substance abuse. Become educated about substance abuse, so you can avoid becoming a victim. Of course, stay clear of using illegal drugs and always drink responsibly. Getting drunk or high can put your life and the lives of others at risk, and the poor decisions you make in a diminished capacity can be embarrassing and have serious consequences, so think carefully before you do either one. Also bear in mind that, as a student-athlete, you are responsible for whatever you consume, including supplements and performance-enhancing drugs (PEDs).

As you learn to balance your lifestyle, continue to focus your talents and energy on who you want to become. Living with a sense of purpose and moderation can enhance your chances of success and give you a greater feeling of personal fulfillment along the way. Realize that positive changes do not necessarily happen quickly. You often have to make a special effort to build up the positives in your life because of the seeming endless presence of negative images, voices, and ideas in society. Stay patient, positive, and consistent because the benefits of a better lifestyle can last a lifetime.

Remember, don't go "out of bounds" when you're off the field.

ONE-ON-ONE

- What are the main sources of stress for you? How can you reduce them?

- What key areas in your social life do you need to keep in check?

- Do you treat your body well enough for you to perform regularly at or near your best? If not, what changes must you make?

- What are some risks of using alcohol or drugs?

- What are PEDs? How can they harm you?

CROSS-TRAIN YOUR BRAIN

I once had a very talented teammate who consistently trained hard during practices. He rarely missed doing anything that could make him become a better athlete. Unfortunately, he did not apply even half that commitment to his studies. He was intelligent, although not naturally book smart, but he hardly went to his classes or did schoolwork. Many mornings when I dropped by his dorm room on my way to classes, I found him curled up under his blanket. Hours later I would knock on his door, only to find him in the same position, but he always transformed into a "beast" for training in the afternoons. Sadly, all his hard training went down the drain because of injury and academic ineligibility. I am convinced that if he had simply gone to his classes and done ninety minutes of studying a day that not only would he have avoided perhaps the lowest GPA in a semester that I ever saw, but he could have been a top national contender in his event when he got healthy.

I saw similar behavior from other student-athletes. Some who would go the extra mile in workouts and were warriors at competitions could turn around and be intimidated, lazy, or, worse, quitters, when doing schoolwork. They seemed content to reinforce the stereotype that they were just "jocks" who could only play sports and not be decent students as well. They abandoned the principles that helped them to improve in sports—daily repetition, commitment, self-discipline, and constantly challenging themselves. Frankly, it is stupid to train hard only to forfeit the chance of showing your athletic abilities because you neglect your studies and become academically ineligible.

REALITY CHECK:
Not taking care of your schoolwork severely limits your chances for success in the classroom and can jeopardize your status as a student-athlete.

You can only compete in collegiate sports if you meet the minimum academic requirements set by the NCAA and your school, both of which you need to know. Regardless of your skills and accomplishments, if you can't make the grades, you can't play. This alone should motivate you to get it together in the classroom. Remember, as in athletics, everyone has different academic abilities and rates of progress. Some people are naturally good at schoolwork while others are not, but natural abilities alone don't make you a champion or a good student. That comes from consistently working hard to develop whatever natural gifts you have.

For many who struggle in the classroom, the real problem does not come from being "dumb." Thousands of student-athletes who fail or barely pass their classes have better mental abilities—memories, imagination, and insight—than their grades regularly show. For instance, they can often remember words to hundreds of songs and do well in a variety of nonacademic circumstances that require some intellectual sharpness. However, they don't consistently translate their creativity and competitiveness to their classes where it would benefit them greatly. Often their biggest problem is not that they struggle—everyone struggles with something in life—but that *they don't care enough* to find out or do what it takes to improve as students.

Here is the good news: No matter what type of student you are now, you have the potential to become a better one. This is the reason most schools spend a great deal on academic resources to help their student-athletes improve in the classroom. However, it is your responsibility to make the most of those resources. Using these resources can help you in many ways, including:

Getting better grades—Improving your grades can be the difference between playing and watching from the sidelines due to academic ineligibility. It can also determine if you receive financial aid or remain in college. Even if you are not now facing academic challenges, better grades can help you secure better postgraduate or job opportunities when your application gets reviewed.

Lowering your stress—Better grades and improved study habits usually lead to less anxiety about your academic affairs, such as your eligibility, writing papers, or preparing for exams. This gives you more positive energy to focus on your athletics or other interests.

Developing your life skills—Many skills needed to improve as a student are essential and transferable to other areas of life. For example, improved study habits can help you to become a better competitor because you can evaluate the game or your opponents more effectively. Good writing skills or being a quick study can also help you with career advancements later in life. Becoming a better student also prepares you to do well in many other life circumstances; for instance, learning how to listen more attentively can help in your relationships.

AIM TO DO WELL ACADEMICALLY

REALITY CHECK:
How you consistently approach your studies usually determines how well you will perform academically.

When you study without proper focus, you will probably not perform up to your best in the classroom. Studying is "brain work." It usually requires your full attention so that you can properly understand and remember the material. If you take your studies seriously, you will likely do better because you actively engage your mind to learn. Approaching your schoolwork with the right frame of mind is important to success, especially in subject areas where you are naturally weaker or have lower interest levels, so that you don't fall behind.

If you currently have a hard time in the classroom, you may first need to shake off negative comments or poor self-confidence about your academic ability and start believing that you can do better. Like overcoming poor athletic performances, making this positive mental switch may not be easy at first, but it is often the key to improvement. Adopting a patient, positive, no-nonsense attitude toward your schoolwork will help you to become a better student.

Over the next few pages, I will share some of the "secrets" that helped me to improve as a student and to do well in the classroom, which I hope can do the same for you.

EVALUATE YOURSELF AS A STUDENT

Earlier in the book, I touched on how you can assess yourself as a student. In addition to those tips, I suggest that you complete this evaluation with the help of your academic advisors. Even though they likely have access to your transcripts, you still should be completely honest with them and yourself about your academic history and habits. They need this information so they can evaluate you accurately as a student and suggest the most appropriate resources and changes in your study habits for you to improve in the classroom. Being evaluated may also allow them to determine whether you have a learning disability, such as dyslexia or attention deficit disorder (ADD), requiring special attention or alternative teaching or testing methods.

CHOOSE THE BEST MAJOR FOR YOU

If you want to enjoy your studies and do well in the classroom, then choose the best major for you. Your choice of major often affects your overall college experience because it can influence your grades, your academic eligibility, and how you feel about yourself and your future. For example, if you struggle in your major, you will likely feel overwhelmed and unsure about your academic fate, which can cause you to lose focus in other areas, such as your athletics. Of course, if you fail too many classes, you will become academically ineligible to compete. Choosing the best major for you not only reduces this uncertainty but also sets you up to get better grades.

I suggest that whatever major you choose should be in a subject area in which you have a strong personal interest, passion, and natural aptitude. In other words, be guided by what you genuinely want to do and what you are naturally good at doing. It also should be manageable and, although not necessary, in an area that allows you to be employable soon after graduation, especially if you have to repay student loans.

Unfortunately many student-athletes choose majors that are not the best ones for them. These majors are ones that they don't enjoy studying, which causes them to struggle academically, or that limit their employability. They may do this to please or follow others, because of misinformation about a degree field, or due to misgivings about their own interests and abilities. Sometimes student-athletes make these choices simply to meet NCAA deadlines for declaring majors.

Like thousands of other college students, you may enter college unsure about what you want to do when you "grow up," so choosing the best major for you is not straightforward. I was in that boat for my first year and a half of college. Fortunately my father gave me some useful tips. First, he suggested that I take a variety of courses to see where my interests and natural abilities lay. Second, he told me to aim at doing well in every course so that I kept my options open. Then he recommended that I choose a major that allowed me to juggle my studies and athletics without too much stress. I followed his advice, and after going back and forth between a few options, I finally chose to earn a degree in business administration.

I truly enjoyed studying my major because it challenged me in different ways, it always kept my interest, and it was manageable. This contributed greatly to my success in the classroom, which freed me to do well in other areas, particularly athletics, and to have time to pursue my other interests, like church involvement. Studying my major also equipped me with many useful tools for the real world after I graduated.

Regardless of your abilities as a student or your confidence about your future, spend time doing proper background work before declaring a major. This includes evaluating yourself as a student; thinking about your interests and passions; speaking with your family, coaches, academic advisors, and professors; and researching the marketplace of your potential degree field choices. Always listen to good advice before declaring your major, but understand that you cannot please everyone.

REALITY CHECK:
If you are not comfortable with your choice of major, then you will likely struggle academically, which may affect other parts of your life.

If you have already declared a major and you presently struggle in it or you discover that your interest is in another subject area, you may consider changing your major. Be aware that changing your major after some time can cause you more problems, such as becoming ineligible to compete because you lack enough core course credit hours to meet minimum NCAA progress-toward-degree requirements or shifting your graduation date. Always talk with your academic advisors and coaches before you change your major. Depending on your circumstances, they may recommend that you change majors or they may suggest ways for you to "tough it out" in your current one. Remember, millions of people work or do postgraduate studies in areas unrelated to their undergraduate degrees, so take heart. Hopefully using some of the study tips in this book and accessing your school's academic resources can help you to finish strong, whatever your major is.

CREATE THE BEST CLASS SCHEDULE FOR YOU

Always visit with your academic advisors before registering for your classes so that you can create a class schedule that works best for you. This schedule should help you to advance quickly toward your degree and to juggle your other demands or goals, mainly your athletic commitments. Aim for a good mix of challenging and easier courses, including core courses for your major and electives. Besides talking with academic advisors, you should ask other students about the best professors to take for particular subjects. Bear in mind that an "easy" class may not be the best one for you to take, especially if the professor is not a good teacher. You may get a good grade in that class but not learn essential information needed to do well in later, harder courses.

At most schools, student-athletes can preregister for courses so that they can make the best class schedule to manage their studies and athletics. Don't take this for granted and wait until the last moment to register for your classes because you could end up unsuccessfully competing against regular students for the last open slots in some courses. Do your best to avoid a poor class schedule, such as one with time conflicts between your classes and your training or with too many tough classes in one day, because it can stress and drain you.

I made my first class schedule in college without much input from my academic advisor. Scheduling evening classes on four nights of the week after training was a huge mistake! I usually had to skip parts of my workouts, mainly the weightlifting program and postworkout training room treatments, so that I could rush back to my dorm room, shower, "cook" (microwaveable rice and tuna), eat, and head out to my classes. It was often difficult to focus well during those classes because of fatigue from the tough workouts, and studying after those classes was tougher. Later that semester, after finding out about my crazy class schedule, my coach "strongly advised" me not to do that again. He was a little late; I had figured that out after the first week of the semester.

Sometimes you may have an unfavorable class schedule or tough classes. In such cases, you will likely have to manage your time better or get some academic help if you want to do well. Dropping a class may also be an option in some circumstances, but you should first talk with your academic advisors to see how it could affect your academic eligibility. I once had to drop a class with a professor who had no sympathy for student-athletes. Even though I was up front about my competition travel schedule, she said that she would penalize me for missing classes on those days. She was also unwilling to let me take exams at any times other than what was on the syllabus, even when I offered to take them earlier. After a month of hell in that class, I talked with my coach and my academic advisors who also agreed that I should drop that class before it ruined my GPA. I retook that course with another professor the following semester, as well as did extra credit hours to make up for that dropped class.

Always get proper advice before doing anything that could affect your academic eligibility, such as not taking enough core courses, dropping classes, or getting an incomplete in a course. Making a good class schedule can often help you to avoid these situations.

SET THE TONE FROM THE START OF EACH SEMESTER

Shaking off the mental cobwebs after your holidays can be hard, but setting the tone for your studies from the start of each semester, especially during your competition semesters, is important. I did this by creating a routine that got me into the groove of being a student from day one of the semester. Actually I started getting my mind ready to be a student again a few days before my holidays ended so the transition would be smoother.

Bear in mind that as the semester continues, your schoolwork and athletics will become more challenging, and distractions tend to increase. Work hard toward doing well in your first assignments or exams in each class so that you can start with good grades. Remember, it is much easier to start the semester with some wiggle room in your grades than to be scrambling at the end trying to improve them.

REALITY CHECK:
Your grades will suffer if you don't make schoolwork your main priority during the semester.

Even your athletics should not regularly take precedence over your schoolwork, especially when you have important work to finish. Being an athlete is *never* a good reason for you to fall behind in your studies. Even though road trips, big competitions, or other important events can interrupt your study routine, always try to do your schoolwork first and on time. This takes pressure off you academically so you can focus on whatever else you want or need to do.

Eventually you will have conflicts in your schedule, mainly because you have too much to do and too little time to do everything. Sometimes your coaches or teammates, who should know better, may pressure you to sacrifice your studies to do other things. If this happens, you will have to make tough choices about prioritizing your schoolwork. Some of these choices may not be popular, and they can become the source of tension with others, but handling your schoolwork first is always in your best long-term interest.

During my first few road trips as a freshman, I struggled to study well when so much was going on around me, including the hectic schedule of traveling and competing and socializing with teammates and friends attending other schools after competitions. I often had to scramble to catch up on my schoolwork when I returned from road trips. Something had to change. I figured out that I studied more productively when I was at home, so I decided not to do important or challenging schoolwork on the road, if possible. Instead I tried to do as much studying as I could before road trips and immediately after I returned. Because schoolwork was my top priority during the week, I could focus more on competing on the weekend with fewer worries about my grades.

If you have to miss several consecutive days of classes for tournaments or championships, then you need to ensure that studying on your road trips is a priority. I know that this is not easy, but you never want to fall too far behind in your schoolwork. I suggest that during your downtime, when you are not traveling, training, or competing, you set aside specific times and places to study, perhaps somewhere quiet in your hotel. Consider rooming with someone who is also serious about schoolwork or who respects your study times. Remember, don't stop being a student just because you are away from school. There's more than enough time for you to both compete well and do some studying on road trips.

MAKE THE MOST OF CLASS TIME

Although a significant part of your studying should be during your private time, class time is valuable, especially when you have a good instructor or the material is difficult. Here are suggestions for getting the most from the time you spend in class:

Go to class—As obvious as this seems, amazingly, many student-athletes regularly skip their classes and wonder why they have poor grades. Going to class is important to academic success. Most instructors use class times to talk about course material, some of which may not be in the textbook. In class, they often explain subjects in a more interactive way and in greater depth. Some professors even make class attendance or participation part of the final grade, so it makes sense to turn up for some "free" or "easy" points. Your coaches may also make class attendance mandatory. In these cases, skipping classes without a valid reason could have negative consequences for you besides your grades.

Come prepared—Coming to class prepared sets you up to learn. Try to review your notes or read ahead for each class, even if it's just for a few minutes before the class starts instead of just socializing with others. Mentally switching gears between your classes makes it easier to shift to the right frame of mind for each subject. Have whatever materials you need for each class—a laptop, notebook, textbook, or pens—readily available so you are not distracted by looking for them during the lecture. These preparations create a posture of learning from the start of the class.

Sit for success—Sit where you can clearly see and hear your instructor and the teaching materials, such as a projector screen or blackboard. Avoid sitting near distractions, such as hallway doors or other heavy traffic or noisy areas. Sometimes that means not sitting next to certain friends so that you can focus better.

Stay attentive—Staying attentive in class helps you to understand the subject better. You will miss far less information when you focus on the instructor. Perhaps the biggest key to staying attentive during class is to come to class with the intention of learning as much as you can. Apply to your classes the same attitudes and focus that you bring to your daily practice sessions.

Take good notes—Good note taking is one of the most useful tools you can have in your academic toolbox. Relying solely on memory can fail you, especially when you face a lot of material or challenging subject matter, or you are under pressure. Taking accurate, clear, and comprehensive notes allows you to review information quickly and easily, which can be useful in preparing for exams or writing papers. Developing a good shorthand system for note taking, such as using certain symbols or abbreviations for words or concepts, helps you to write down more information and miss less of your lecture.

Ask questions—School is a place of learning, so no one expects you to know or understand everything about every subject taught. Most people have a fear of being embarrassed by asking a "dumb question" during class. However, it is far "dumber" to remain in silent ignorance and potentially miss understanding the lecture.

If this fear paralyzes you or the time is not appropriate to ask the instructor for clarification, you may have to take other steps. For example, you may be able to ask a classmate for a quick explanation without disrupting others in the class, or you may wait until after class to ask one of the better students in the class or the instructor for clarification. Do your best to understand whatever is not clear as soon as possible so you have one less thing to worry about later. Asking questions and clarifying information may be considered forms of participation by some professors and often benefit others in your class too.

Participate—Try to participate in class or review discussions. The different perspectives or explanations that emerge as you voice your views and hear those of others can deepen your understanding or clarify misunderstandings about topics. Sometimes you may be wrong or others may not agree with you; this is all part of learning and interacting with others. Take what is useful and discard what is not.

Practice good classroom manners—Learn the rules for every class and follow them. For example, some professors don't mind if you eat during their classes, but others do. The same applies to using your cell phone or laptop. Always respect your instructors and classmates. Come with the right attitude and avoid being rude, outlandish, or disruptive. Remember, your conduct in class matters and will likely be reported to your coach. Here's a bonus tip: Although some of your classes may be scheduled immediately after your workouts, try not to come to class looking or smelling "funky"—that can become an unintentional distraction to others. Seriously.

Create relationships with others—Although most of your friends will likely be other student-athletes, classes provide a setting for you to form relationships with other students or instructors. These relationships can be useful to you for the duration of courses and beyond. They are also great ways to expand your network socially and professionally. More immediately, classmates can help you in many ways, such as providing notes when you have to miss classes for competitions or forming study groups. As with all relationships, never mistreat others, abuse their goodwill, or take them for granted. Most of all, add some value to these relationships by returning help when you can.

SUCCESS TIPS TO IMPROVE YOUR STUDY HABITS

Develop a consistent routine—As in your athletic training, having a consistent study routine conditions your mind and body to doing schoolwork at set times in set locations. Try to develop study routines for when you are at home and on road trips.

Stay organized—Imagine how it would be if you went to training every day and your coaches did not have any structure for practice sessions. It would probably be chaotic and frustrating. Structure is important for success because it gives direction and sets boundaries. Tackling your studies in an organized way brings order, clarity, and focus to your study time, which allows you to study more effectively. Make to-do lists for your study sessions so that you stay on track toward your goals. Keep whatever you need handy, such as notebooks, textbooks, snacks, or water to avoid disrupting your workflow.

Keep your study time sacred—If you plan to study, then study. Set boundaries for yourself and others that clearly communicate that your study time is off-limits to interruptions. Take your studies at least as seriously as you take your workouts. Turn off your cell phone, stop surfing the web and chatting, and get to work. This is important because if you are not mindful, a thirty-second chat can snowball into a five-minute conversation that can change your mood and motivation to study.

REALITY CHECK:
If you don't keep your study time sacred, others won't either.

Find the right atmosphere—The right atmosphere, which includes your physical location, furniture, background noise, and even surrounding people, helps you to study better.

Although some coffee shops and parts of the library may be cool places to hang out, they can be less than ideal study spots, especially if your work is difficult or you are prone to distractions. Also bear in mind that if you are used to studying around constant distractions or noise, you might find it harder to concentrate during an exam in a quiet room. Studying in exam room-like conditions can often best prepare you for the real thing.

Whenever I studied in my dorm room I made sure that I never got too comfortable. I found that studying on my bed usually made me feel sleepy or lazy, so I sat at my desk or on the floor. For more serious work, I went to the library and found a place away from friends and foot traffic, usually a booth in the microfilm section in the basement. I avoided studying with the TV on because sometimes I would unintentionally look at it and end up watching a show instead of concentrating on my work. Although I liked listening to music while I studied, I tried not to play songs that caused me to hum, sing, or lose focus. When the background ambience, like music or other people, started to take my attention away from studying, I changed or stopped it, took a short break, or moved to another place.

Constantly review your work—Reviewing your notes and textbooks improves your understanding and memory of a subject. Repetition reinforces, so try to go over notes from your lectures as soon as possible after classes. This will also improve your readiness for exams, especially pop quizzes, and help when writing papers. I usually underlined or highlighted important material for quick reference later on. Also try to learn from the questions or topics that you missed in your tests or papers.

Aim for productivity—You need to ensure that you are being productive during your study times before you slow down from fatigue, distractions, or loss of concentration.

Even when you hit a mental rut, like reading the same line a few times accidentally or without understanding it, don't let it ruin your session. Try to get help, take a break, or move on to another topic.

My study habits for most of my high school career were not very good. In fact, I could barely study for two hours a day before my brain rebelled and shut down. (Sound familiar to you?) However, in my final years of high school I needed to study much more to prepare for a series of important and difficult cumulative exams. Fortunately, I discovered what I called the "45/15" study method, which I also used in college. Here is how it worked.

Instead of trying to study for two or three hours straight—actually, struggling to hold on after I hit the mental brick wall around ninety minutes—I studied for only forty-five minutes each hour. I then took a fifteen-minute break during which I stretched, took a walk, talked with friends, checked my messages, or got something to eat or drink. I made sure to check my watch regularly so that I could wrap up whatever I was doing in time to get back to studying. When my attention started to decrease after a few hours, I adjusted my study time per hour downward, using a 40/20 or a 30/30 division. I found that using this method—breaking each hour of my study time into work and rest segments—helped me to study more productively and for longer each day. Perhaps this approach can work for you, too.

Be prepared to put in quality time—There is no way around this reality—just as consistently good athletes put quality time into their sport, consistently good students sacrifice in other areas so that they can commit considerable time to their studies. Expect to do the same and plan accordingly if you want better grades. In other words, mandatory study hall alone is not likely to help you become a much better student.

Like many students, I was introduced to CliffsNotes in high school, but soon learned that while they were good tools to get a basic understanding of a subject, they were not replacements for real studying. So I was somewhat wary at first when a friend on the football team claimed to have the "hookup" for an upcoming exam. He said that one of his teammates, who had the same professor at a different class time, had promised to give him a copy of the exam questions. Apparently his teammate's exam was on the day before ours was scheduled. My friend began discreetly but rigorously canvassing all the student-athletes in our class to join him for a "study session" of these questions on the night before our exam. Perhaps he should have been a car salesman because he convinced most of them, and almost me, to come. I remembered my CliffsNotes experiences, and I did not feel comfortable with cheating. Instead, I decided to pass on his offer and did my usual exam review. Good thing I did because after the exam I saw my friend and his not-so-happy band of disciples exiting the exam room looking stunned and panicked. The professor had given our class a completely different exam than the one he gave his other class the previous day.

REALITY CHECK:
Consistently good grades don't come from taking shortcuts; they come from spending quality time studying.

Exercise your mind—Many good coaches continually practice plays, go over films, and discuss game plans with their athletes because they know that improvements don't come when they are in mental autopilot mode. Coaches try to get their athletes to engage in exercises that keep them mentally sharp, which is important to training well and winning tough competitions. Similarly, regular exposure to people and ideas that offer intellectual stimulation will help you to improve as a student. In other words, do more with your free time than gossip, watch movies, or play video games. Try to keep some level of mental stimulation during vacations to benefit you when you return to school. Remember, it is easier to become a better student when you love to learn.

Master the basics—The further you go in college, the harder the work will get. Prepare yourself for more advanced courses by mastering the basics in each subject area. Sometimes you may need to revisit old notes or textbooks or arrange for tutoring. Spend time developing your reading, writing, comprehension, critical thinking, and computer skills, all of which you need to do well academically.

I kept all my notes from my first day of college until I graduated and referred to them whenever I needed to brush up on a subject. I usually wrote out or repeated aloud key definitions and formulas to help me understand and remember material. I also tried to answer the questions at the end of sections in my textbooks because I knew that if I could answer those correctly, then I understood the subject properly.

GO AFTER THE GRADE YOU WANT

Becoming a better student may not always result in getting better grades in some classes. Sometimes you have to know how to work the system to your advantage ("master the playbook.") Let's look at a few more "secrets" that you can use to improve your grades.

The *class syllabus* usually describes how a professor calculates final grades. For example, exams may be worth fifty percent of the final grade, while a term paper may make up twenty percent. Use this information to understand how you are graded as you work toward the grade you want. Focus on doing well in all your graded work but especially in those areas worth more to your final grade.

Monitor your grades throughout the semester so you know if you are on target and whether you need to make adjustments. *Resolve* all grade issues as soon as possible. Professors are less likely to work with you on grades when they are bombarded with grade change requests from other students or they are busy working on their final grade submissions.

At the end of one semester, I was shocked to discover that my final grade in one course was a letter grade lower than all my exams in that class during that semester. I bumped into the professor of that course early in the following semester, and he was surprised to learn about my final grade because he knew how well I did on his exams. He told me to visit his office later in the week to "see what he could do." During that meeting, my excitement soon faded when he informed me that he could not do anything about my grade because I had missed handing in too many of the two-page chapter summaries required at the start of each class. I confessed that I used to ignore those summaries and focused more on exams because I thought that exams were more important. He understood but also regrettably told me that I should have paid closer attention to the syllabus and to my grades during the semester.

Instructors usually evaluate you with various *tests*, such as pop quizzes; multiple-choice or true or false questions; short or long answers to questions; or take-home, open-book, or cumulative exams. Performing well in each of these tests requires different skills. For example, short-answer exams focus on accuracy and brevity, while longer essay type ones require more extensive descriptions or arguments. Cumulative exams demand comprehensive memory of the material for the entire semester, while open-book exams mainly entail knowing where to find the right answers in your textbook or notes. You can prepare more effectively by tweaking your regular study routine according to how you will be tested.

Although you should always take your schoolwork seriously, sometimes *treating your classes like games* can help you improve in them. This gives you a chance to apply the same competitiveness and discipline that you have for your sport to your classes. Try to overcome every obstacle, such as exams, pop quizzes, or assignment that your "opponents" (professors) use to stop you from winning (doing well in their courses). If you want to have a winning record (good grade) at the end of the season (semester), then you constantly have to aim to do well (by preparation and execution) at every competition (test and assignment).

I approached my classes with a simple mind-set: I wanted to "win." For example, on the first day of one course, my professor proudly announced that everyone, including he, would be disappointed by the grades in his course. Of course, I took his words as a personal challenge. Perhaps it's the competitor in me, but I always seemed to perform better whenever someone challenged or trash-talked me. His words motivated me to bring my A game, literally. I went the extra mile in his course. For example, I spoke to some of his former students about how to get better grades in his course, I only missed classes when I had to travel for competitions, I paid special attention and took extensive notes during his lectures, and I studied for his classes more diligently than I did for most of my other courses. It paid off, and he congratulated me for doing much better than he had expected. I earned his respect as a student, and more importantly to me, I earned a good grade in that course.

Treating your classes like games can help you to stay competitive about getting good grades throughout the semester.

MASTER "FACIAL RECOGNITION"

When I was younger, my father sometimes spoke about his students, particularly the ones who made an extra effort to visit during his office hours to talk about his courses or sometimes about themselves. These interactions occasionally influenced how he graded their work. For instance, he was more likely to give the benefit of the doubt or second chances to students who showed genuine interest in doing well in his courses than to those who didn't. I figured out that because professors are human, connecting with that human element—a key component of what I called "facial recognition"—could be beneficial to getting better grades.

By consciously making a regular effort to be recognized and to develop relationships with your professors or teaching assistants, you can move from being just another social security number or name on their registers to being a "real person." Humanizing your desire to succeed in their classes helps to get them on your side. Visit with professors after classes or during their office hours to tell them about your academic or career goals, to give them updates on your travel schedule, and to discuss your progress or challenges in their courses. Do this early and often. Such visits can also provide insight into their biases, potential exam questions, and extra credit opportunities for you.

I worked hard on "facial recognition" in college. At the start of each semester I tried to let my professors know who I was by name and by face. I also wanted them to know about my interest in doing well in their courses and that, even though I was a student-athlete, I planned to work hard for my grades.

I told them that I needed their help to succeed, and I made an effort to inform them about when I would have to miss their classes for road trips and about how I was doing in their courses. Most of them appreciated my honesty, ambition, and effort. Many would suggest ways that I could achieve my goals, mainly through extra credit opportunities in their classes, and some even recommended which professors I should take for future courses. Apart from studying hard, much of my success in the classroom was because of "facial recognition" and carefully using the goodwill I developed with my professors.

If you have played sports for a while, you probably know this simple rule: If you want more playing time, you have to give your coaches what they want. Getting good grades in your classes is no different: *Give your professors what they want.* Professors usually hint or speak openly about their preferences on subjects during classes—note what these are. I used to jot them down in the margins of my notebooks for easy review later on. Sometimes it is easier to get the grade you want by accommodating their preferences or biases, whether those involve agreeing with their points of view, format of a paper, conduct in class, or use of e-mail for communication. Quid pro quo: Give them what they want to get the grade you want.

PREPARE TO DO WELL

As a student-athlete, how you perform in the classroom matters. The NCAA requires that you not only pass your classes and maintain a minimum GPA but also comply with its progress-toward-degree rules. In other words, you can't load up on electives and not take core courses in your declared major. Your school may have even higher academic requirements that you must fulfill before you are academically eligible to compete for them.

You will benefit by making full use of whatever academic resources are at your disposal before, and especially when, you face academic challenges. Apply whatever ways you use to learn about something that interests you, such as researching it on the Internet, asking questions, or watching related TV shows, to help you become a better student.

By focusing on being a better student, you will likely avoid academic problems, have less stress, and earn better grades, which could help when applying for jobs or postgraduate positions. Remember that the skills needed to be a good student, such as staying organized, aiming for productivity, and exercising your mind, are life skills, which transfer to many nonacademic areas of your life.

As with everything else you do, challenge yourself to be the best student that you can be, and be willing to work consistently toward improvement. Make your schoolwork your main priority, and do your best to keep it at the top of your daily to-do list. Although you may find studying a challenge, especially when so many other people and activities fight for your time and attention, studying prepares you to do well in the classroom. You may also find it helpful to treat your classes as games and use your creativity and competitiveness to "win." Try to form relationships with your professors and always be mindful of what they want from you as a student.

I strongly recommend that, in addition to applying the "secrets" in this book, you take the time to research and use other resources—books, articles, or programs—designed to help you improve as a student. Rest assured, the focus, sacrifices, and commitment you invest to become better in the classroom will pay off now and after college. Remember, don't just train your body; train your brain as well.

ONE-ON-ONE

- What happens when your studies are not a top priority in your life?

- What steps can you take to become a better student?

- What three things should you consider when choosing the best major for you?

- Name four ways that you can make the most of your class time.

- Besides treating your classes like "games," what other methods can you use to get the grades you want?

DEVELOP A CHAMPION MIND-SET

Champions usually enter competitions as "winners." This became evident to me just before winning my first NCAA Championships title in my junior year at the NCAA Indoor Championships. During the break between the semifinals and finals of the 200-meter dash, a high school friend came over to chat. He approached me beaming because he had qualified for the NCAA Championships for the first time—his school's relay squad was the last team accepted into the competition. In contrast, I was already a six-time All-American. While he felt happy just to be there, I arrived absolutely focused on winning my first NCAA title.

During our conversation, he said something that struck me. After seeing my qualifying races, he said that I looked ready to be the national champion. Of course, I felt the same, but that was the first time someone had mentally evaluated me in my "zone." About two hours later, I would prove us both correct, breaking Michael Johnson's NCAA record on the way to winning the title. Later that evening, I watched my friend's relay squad struggle and be eliminated because they ran worse than expected. When we spoke after the competition, he confessed that qualifying for the Championships felt like winning the title for them. Although I understood the feeling, it was clear that they could not win because they did not come to the competition as champions. While not impossible, winning becomes more difficult when you don't enter a competition already feeling like the winner. In the following pages, we will look at a few things that can help you develop a champion mind-set and the tools to back it up.

EXERCISE YOUR WILL TO WIN

Relying on athletic talent alone may be enough to win big in high school but not in college; certainly not in larger conferences or at the national level. Collegiate athletes in big games or championships often have similar talent levels, so natural athletic abilities usually play a lesser role when facing tougher competition. Although having the right training, equipment, opportunities, and prechampionship competitions are important in becoming a championship-caliber athlete, there are other factors that influence whether you will win.

REALITY CHECK:
If you want to win the "big ones" in college, you have to bring more to the table than your dreams and natural athletic talent.

How well you have prepared and how well you use what you have against your opponents determine your results. Winners execute the best game plan at the right time. Legendary basketball coach Bobby Knight said that most people have the will to win; few have the will to prepare to win. A friend who was a multiple NCAA champion and later a world champion once explained to me that this was his secret to winning the "big ones." Although most athletes dream about winning a championship title, how many have a consistent will to do what it takes—the big and small things—to get to the top?

Champions feel confident about the results before they lace up to compete and for good reason. Competitions provide the perfect time for them to showcase their talents, outperform competitors, and confirm what they already know—they are winners. When the time to perform arrives, their fears and anxieties dissolve, they put on their game face, and the drive to win takes over.

At heart, most champions are disciplined competitors with the drive to do whatever it takes to be number one. Although individual characteristics and strengths vary, here's a basic profile of a champion athlete.

A Champion Athlete

- Loves to win and hates to lose.
- Is proactive about winning.
- Is fearless about winning.
- Finds ways to win.
- Creates good game plans.
- Stays focused on the tasks at hand.
- Handles the pressures of the moment best.
- Takes advantage of whatever opportunities are available to improve.
- Makes the fewest mistakes when it counts most.
- Creates opportunities for strengths to shine and minimizes the effects of weaknesses.
- Enjoys competing against tough opponents and overcoming odds.

- Exploits opponents' weaknesses.
- Feels like a champion before the competition starts.

Consider this list and look at yourself carefully. Do you have what it takes to be a champion? Does this list shed light on how you can perform up to your true potential?

GET YOUR MIND RIGHT BEFORE YOU COMPETE

Mental preparation and toughness also separate could-be champions from actual champions. Winners master those internal conversations, such as "I can do it" or "I cannot do it," before they compete, while others do not. Champions "know" they are winners before their events start and confidently answer all questions about their readiness to win. In contrast, other athletes may have all the physical tools or may outwardly look the part of a champion but have lingering questions about their preparation and abilities to pull it off before and during competitions. This chorus of unanswered questions or mental baggage often distracts them and gives opponents a window of opportunity to exploit.

For most of my senior year, I was not as focused as I should have been. I was doing a poor job at juggling too many things in my life, from my personal relationships to injuries and sickness that almost wiped out my outdoor season. Although I had a decent season by my high standards, I was mentally and emotionally on cruise control at most competitions. I recall waking up on the morning of my last Outdoor Conference Championships and feeling "out of it." I told my roommate that I would have happily stayed under the covers all day if I was not the cocaptain of our team and if it was not my last Conference Championships. My main rival apparently had no such issues.

He got a step on me in the 100-meter dash and held on for the slightest victory against my late charge. That defeat was my first individual loss at a Conference Championships since I was a freshman. The stadium was in shock because even though that race was predicted to be a dogfight, most people expected me to emerge with the "W." It got worse. After I got out to a huge lead in my favored event, the 200-meter dash, the same guy ran me down only meters away from the finish line. By the end of the day I was 0-3 versus him, as his relay squad also defeated my team earlier in the day. As if the embarrassment of losing so spectacularly was not enough, some football players from the host school booed me from the stands as I walked out of the stadium with my coach. Apparently they had lost some money by betting on me.

With less than two weeks to prepare for our rematch at the NCAA Outdoor Championships my mind finally switched "on." Over the next ten days, I put together arguably the best series of workouts in my college career in anticipation of our epic showdown. I knew a lot would be on the line.

Because I had multiple rounds in my events at the Championships, I chose to cruise through my 200-meter dash semifinal. Later that evening, my roommate confessed that he was a little worried because my would-be nemesis looked impressive while comfortably winning his semifinal heat. In contrast to my nonchalant mind-set two weeks before, I confidently told my roommate that it would take a world-leading performance in that event to defeat me . . . and I was still not going to lose! The next day, for the first time in many months, I lined up with my mind set totally on executing and winning, and that I did in memorable fashion.

Even though champions may not have the most talent or the best physical preparation, they make their minds and bodies work together better than all their competitors when it counts. Entering a competition mentally prepared helps you to deal better with everything happening both inside and outside of you. It also provides a sense of calm and direction so you can visualize executing your game plan.

In addition to their main purpose of getting you physically in shape, training sessions offer the best times to get your mind right for competitions. Training helps you to work through difficulties, put your game plan together, and improve your mind-body connection away from the pressures of competition.

Sometimes training alone is not enough to get you to the next level, and you may need to seek some outside help, such as from a sports psychologist or a peak performance coach, to unlock the mental doors between your current performance and your true potential. Although sports psychology has recently gained greater acceptance in the sporting world, some athletes and coaches still consider it to be unnecessary, a sign of weakness, or taboo. Like me, you may benefit from working with someone to improve your mental game.

I visited with a sports psychologist at one point because I was having problems dealing with the steep falloff in my performances at the end of my freshman season. To be honest, I was skeptical at first, but by the end of the session, I had acquired some tools that helped me to clear out some of the mental debris that was affecting my performances. I also learned some useful breathing techniques that allowed me to refocus my positive energy and to stay calm when negative thoughts flooded my mind before and during competitions. If you are really struggling to translate your training to your competitions, then consider talking with your coach about getting this or a similar type of help.

REALITY CHECK:
You have a better chance of executing your best performance when you properly prepare and synchronize your mind and body.

PERFECT PRACTICE MAKES PERFECT

Practice alone does not make perfect, but it does make permanent. If you want to reinforce perfect or near flawless execution, then you must train to do so. In other words, perfect practice makes perfect. What you consistently repeat at practice will inevitably show up under the stress of competition. Constantly training with poor habits and attitudes leads to poor or subpar performances. For example, if you usually quit or work less hard during tough workouts, you will likely do the same when competitions heat up. In fact, the only thing that you learn to do well when you regularly give up is how to quit. Similarly, if you usually have a negative attitude in training, you will probably be negative when competing. Sloppiness in training translates to sloppiness in competitions.

Always come to training ready to learn—this is what practice is really about. I know this is not always easy, especially when your practice sessions are early in the morning or immediately before or after your classes, but developing your ability to be "present" and focused during workouts prepares you to get the most from them. Also learn to do each drill, exercise, and play consistently and properly. This may mean asking your coach or teammates for help or slowing it down to get it right.

REALITY CHECK:
If you cannot consistently do it correctly during training, you won't consistently get it right in competition.

Pay special attention to details and to perfecting the fundamentals of your event or position. This will help you to become more efficient, reduce your chance of injury, and decrease variances in your performances. You will become a better athlete when you add speed, power, and intensity to proper fundamentals.

Many athletes talk about "stepping it up" or "taking it to the next level" at big competitions when they are in the spotlight and everything is on the line. News flash: For most, when the pressure gets too high, the only "next level" is down. Why? Because you most often revert to what you know or usually do when you are under pressure. Forcing your body to work significantly past its regular training levels or your current technical abilities often backfires. You cannot expect your body to perform at the next level without preparation. Even though visualizing a great performance helps, pushing your body to get there without the proper background work may cause serious injury to you and your ego.

Most champions understand that, as a rule, they cannot consistently outperform their training, so they don't train haphazardly or with a carefree attitude, or rely on luck to win. They work hard not to leave any loose ends for opponents to exploit. Although they "save something" for competitions, they don't save it all during training. They also do not overtrain or leave their best performances on the practice field. Instead, they usually have extraordinary work ethics and constantly push themselves at practice. For them, the "next level" is a logical extension of their workouts, not much different from how they regularly train and certainly not a radical increase in intensity and stress. Their competition results usually confirm what they do in training.

REALITY CHECK:
Exceptional performances start with
exceptional training. If you want to improve
your competition results, first improve
your training.

MAKE YOUR "BAD" GOOD AND "GOOD" GREAT

In high school, everyone knew the pattern of my races: poor starts, great finishes. Although I was successful, disciplined, and driven, I often relied on my finishing strength and did not spend enough time improving my main weakness, my start. This worked most times because I could run down competitors in the last few meters of races. Although I knew my start needed improvement, my motivation to give it more attention remained low because, frankly, I kept winning. As the saying goes, "If it ain't broke, don't fix it."

The summer before I came to college, a local club coach gave me some advice that challenged this view and how I trained. He told me that if I wanted to do well after high school, I needed to make my "bad" good and my "good" great. He warned me that as I advanced in my athletic career, I would face tougher competitors. When I competed against them, a bad start could mean the difference between winning, losing, or being eliminated. He added that although I might never become the *best* starter, by becoming a *good* starter, I could stay in striking distance and have a better chance of overcoming better starters with my superior finish.

My seventh-place finish at the NCAA Indoor Championships in the 55-meter dash during my freshman season made me face the reality of what I needed to do if I wanted to win the "big one." The following year, my start improved, and I finished third at that meet. I moved up one place to second during my junior year, and by my senior season, I had set the NCAA and world records in the event. Although I was never first out of the starting blocks, the work that I had put into overcoming this weakness allowed me to gain ground on my opponents sooner in my races, putting me in a better position to win.

To become great at anything, you must first become consistently good at it. Most athletes rely on their strengths. They like to remain in their comfort zone. Sometimes, they do not spend enough time working on weaknesses because they do not know what their weaknesses are, they underestimate the impact of those weaknesses on their performance, or they don't think that they could improve in those areas. Their weaknesses create disadvantages that their strengths may not overcome under pressure or when competing against more talented, disciplined, and driven athletes.

Champions dig deeper to identify their strengths and weaknesses and consistently work on expanding and balancing their skills, and preparing their game plan *before* they enter the arena. They also work to reduce competitors' advantages, often by learning how to exploit competitors' "soft spots" and neutralize their opponents' strengths. Champions also focus on improving weaker areas to support their strengths.

Remember, your weaknesses will persist if you lack the dedication to perfect your total game. Weaknesses often separate winners from losers. If you want to be a champion, you must not only make your "good" great, but also, and perhaps more importantly, you need to make your "bad" good. This quality separates talented athletes from champions.

COMPETE TO WIN

Before every competition I psyched myself up to win. For example, two of my favorite precompetition mantras were "Why not me?" and "Why should someone else win?" I always repeated these under my breath to remind myself that until the results became official, I needed to fight as hard as I could for as long as I could to win. Sometimes I would repeat them during a race to jolt myself back into the "moment" when I temporarily lost focus. Whenever I did not win, I needed to know that at least I had given it my all trying to be victorious. Although I always felt happy "just to be there," I always felt happier to win.

I had a teammate who had all the physical tools to be one of the best in the nation in his event. He could go toe-to-toe with anyone at training, including NCAA champions. If the NCAA had Practice All-Americans, he would be on the First Team because no one could out-train him. Unfortunately, he usually transformed between training and competition, and he never brought the killer instinct that made him so good at practice to competitions. Instead he spent more time worrying about the rankings and his competitors than simply competing to win. Even with his immense physical gifts and a solid training program, he hardly won and finished his career arguably far less accomplished than he should have.

Many athletes compete for reasons other than winning, such as to set new personal bests, to please others, or to help out their team. Although some of these reasons may have merit, regardless of circumstances, your win-loss record, and your opponents, you will often achieve much more when you just go for the win. Even when it seems like a long shot, don't sell yourself short or give up all your hard work prematurely without a good fight.

**REALITY CHECK:
You can't win if you quit making
plays or if you fear losing.**

Many incredible upsets and comebacks have happened because players had die-hard attitudes when they were down or the odds were against them. You may surprise yourself and others when you keep a positive and winning attitude until the game or event is officially over. Remember, have fun and enjoy the privilege of competing, but always go for the win.

FOCUS ON EXECUTION

In high school, I once competed against someone who wore the flashiest warm-ups and competition gear I had ever seen. After finishing dead last, he jokingly declared: "If you can't win, then look pretty!" Judging by the crowd's response, he got what he wanted—attention but not the win.

Although many champions care about how they look and what happens around them, their priorities change dramatically during competitions. In the heat of battle, their consuming focus is on executing the right strategy, at the right time, and in the right way. Champions also tend to avoid or reduce distractions when it is time to compete. They deal with everyone and everything else not directly associated with winning *after* they have done their job. In other words, who is there, what they are wearing or doing, and anything else not immediately related to competing at that moment are secondary.

I could often tell which teammates were ready to compete well by what they packed for road trips. Those who came for business usually packed light, bringing their competition gear, toiletries, schoolwork, and a few other essentials. The ones who were not as focused on competing frequently traveled with more stuff than they needed, such as multiple changes of clothing for after parties and excessive movies and video games; some even forgot to pack their competition equipment! They seemed more interested in socializing and spectating than on taking care of business on the field, and their performances usually confirmed this.

Remember, the fewer distractions you have before and during a competition, the easier it is to focus on executing.

DEVELOP YOUR PLAN Bs

Most athletes can do well when things work in their favor, but what happens when things do not? How many can still perform well in less than perfect situations? Far fewer. They don't handle contingencies or "curveballs" well because they don't foresee or prepare for them properly.

During most big competitions, athletes must deal with less than ideal circumstances like changes in schedules, bad weather, or unexpected opponents. Champions win because they know how to perform well, or at least better than others, under challenging conditions. Winners have alternative plans if their first option or ideal situations are not possible. They patiently and confidently make the right changes so that the momentum swings their way. In contrast, most other athletes do not have or practice other workable options or they lack the confidence to function in Plan B mode. So they often panic and fail to make the right plays needed to win.

At my last NCAA Indoor Championships, I entered the competition as the NCAA record-holder and defending champion in the 200-meter dash. After winning my semifinal race in that event, I returned to the warm-up area for a short nap before the finals about two hours later. When the alarm on my watch sounded, I popped up and started to do my final warm-up, but within a few strides, I felt a cramp in my calf. At first I did not worry because that sometimes happened during training. I figured that I would walk it off or let the trainer stretch it out while I rehydrated with electrolytes. When I jogged back to the trainer, I felt my other calf spasm. I could not believe that I had cramps in both calves one hour before my title defense.

I walked slowly toward my coach, trying not to let any competitors see my grimace from the pain. Of course, when I told him about my situation, his face immediately flushed red because of my "bad luck" from injuries and foolish tactical mistakes at previous NCAA Championships. I reassured him that although my cramps were serious, I would be able to compete. During the next thirty minutes, I drank lots of liquids while the trainer vigorously worked to provide some relief. I managed a very short and cautious warm-up before they called for all the finalists in my event to assemble. I went through the last bit of race strategy with my coach, and we both shrugged because we knew that it would be touch-and-go. Nothing guaranteed that my calves would not spasm at any moment, especially under the stress of the finals.

As usual, I said my prayers and went out to the starting line with the other competitors. I set my starting blocks but did not take practice starts because I feared that any explosive action before the final could end it for me. I originally entered the Championships wanting to challenge my NCAA record, but given the sudden changes in my circumstances, I felt quite happy to retain my title with a conservative and controlled performance.

I stayed calm and operated in Plan B mode because I had faced similar situations in practice. I knew what it was like to finish workouts with cramps in my calves and how to run that event several different ways. I also knew that, based on my preparation, I was physically and mentally ready to win. How much success you have as an athlete depends on how well you consistently anticipate and prepare for eventualities before you compete, and on how well you execute your game plan in imperfect circumstances during competitions. Mastering Plan Bs is not only smart but often necessary to outperform opponents when the pressure comes.

Spend time researching what competitors and circumstances you may face during competition, such as the weather conditions or the competition venue, so you can prepare alternative plans accordingly. Preferably do this with your coach so you are on the same page, especially if you play a team sport. Doing this can calm you and help you to stay focused, whatever you have to face. Having good Plan Bs gives you better control over more factors that influence how well you perform. Remember, when you spend too much time worrying about what you cannot control, you start losing control of what you can.

GO THE EXTRA MILE

Winners go the extra mile to succeed while others are prepared to give only minimal or ordinary effort.

REALITY CHECK:
When you truly believe in yourself
and commit to reaching your goals,
finding the time and making the sacrifices
to do so become easier.

Here are some common "extra mile" areas to give you an edge over your competitors that many student-athletes overlook:

Be a student of the game—Learn about the history of your sport and develop your skill set and strategies. For example, watch films, read books, magazine, or articles about your sport or event, ask questions, and always look out for tips that can help you to become better.

Eat and sleep right—Give your mind and body a chance to perform at their best by increasing your energy, focus, and recovery.

Warm up and cool down properly—Get your mind and body in sync before and after workouts and competitions. Doing these also can decrease your chances of injury and improve your recovery time.

Stay in the training room—Do preventative maintenance, such as icing, massages, and taping. Learn the difference between normal pain and signs of possible injury and take steps to remain healthy.

Stay on top of injuries—Be consistent and proactive about doing your rehab, and be aggressive but don't rush it. Give your team doctor, trainers, and coaches early and honest feedback about your condition so that they can create the best rehab program for you.

Get serious in the weight room—Improve your explosive power, strength, and core stability. These can better your performance while reducing your chance of injury and burnout, especially when you play a physical contact sport, have to compete in multiple events, or have a long season.

Do extra stretching—Fifteen minutes of extra stretching every day, perhaps while watching TV, and especially immediately after training, can significantly improve your flexibility and mobility, as well as aid in your recovery.

Stay sharp during your holidays—Continually work on your physical fitness, understanding of the game, and skills, rather than letting them rust. What you do in the off-season often affects how well you perform during the season.

CHAMPION MIND-SET

By the end of my college career, I knew that few competitors could defeat me when I was at my best. They had to bring their A game during the season and their A+ game at championships. Besides developing my physical abilities, I consistently worked hard on going the extra mile so I could be a step ahead of my opponents. For example, I was more interested in getting tips from famous professional athletes who happened to attend some of my competitions than getting their autographs or pictures. I also spent hundreds of hours developing my relationship with my coach, watching film, and finding out whatever I could about my events. I tried to learn from both my victories and my losses. After each competition, I did a review with my coach to discuss what I needed to improve and how best to make those improvements. I let the disappointments of losing and the pursuit of a perfect performance motivate me to train and do better at my next competition.

Every summer, I sacrificed hanging out with my family and friends at home so that I could compete internationally for my country. This was extremely challenging and tiring after my long collegiate season. However, it gave me more chances to learn my event and to perfect my skills against some of the best athletes in the world, while many of my collegiate competitors were at their homes getting rusty or out of shape.

I also became smarter about monitoring my body and being up front with my coach and trainers about health issues. Of course, I was not perfect. I should have eaten better, rested more, and been more devoted to my weight program. Overall, I knew that when it was time to compete, all I needed to do was to execute my game plan properly and I would perform well.

YOU CAN'T OUTPERFORM YOUR TRAINING

Although natural ability is definitely an important factor in winning, perhaps the most significant factor is how you handle your opponents and various conditions at competition time. If you want to be a champion, you must first realize that you cannot consistently outperform your training. You also need to assess your abilities and work on making your "bad" (weaknesses) good and your "good" (strengths) great.

You need to think and train like a champion at all times to become a champion. That means preparing properly and making all your workouts count. Workouts provide an opportunity to prepare physically and mentally for the stress of competition. During training sessions, focus on executing what you need to do with few mistakes and always practice the right habits and attitudes so they become second nature. This helps to lower your stress and increases your chances of doing the right things under game-time pressures.

Before and during competitions, keep your focus on what you need to do. Properly executing your game plan is critical to success, especially when circumstances become less than ideal or you have to resort to Plan B or other options. Don't allow negative comments from the media or anonymous posters on blogs or forums to get you off your game. Despite your season results or ranking, how you perform at big games and championships matters most. That's what all your hard training is really about and how you will most likely be remembered. Use your training sessions and prechampionship competitions to get physically, mentally, and emotionally ready to peak then, and leave it all on the field. Always give your best *on that day*, even if it's a tough day at the "office." Never quit!

Of course, although winning is important, how you play the game also matters. For example, you could "win" a game but "lose" your integrity and reputation if you won illegally or in an unsportsmanlike way. In contrast, you could lose a competition but still win the respect of coaches, teammates, fans, and opponents by how you played.

Remember, you win or lose before you compete, so develop and live with a champion mind-set.

ONE-ON-ONE

- Why do champions often feel like winners before they compete?

- How are your practice habits affecting your competition results?

- Besides preparation and athletic ability, what do you need in order to win?

- Name five traits of champion athletes.

- What are four "extra mile" areas that you can use to gain an advantage?

PREPARE FOR THE END ZONE

During my last semester, after a long summer of competing, I struggled to stay focused on my schoolwork. In spite of the extra work I had to put in to finish my double major, I just did not feel motivated. I knew that if I didn't somehow reenergize, my grades would suffer, but frankly, I was burned out and didn't really care. My father must have heard the senioritis in my voice because at the end of one long phone conversation, he told me, "Go out with a bang, not a whimper." I am glad that he did because that was the first semester for which I did not set any academic goals—I simply wanted it to be over. Fortunately, as in many of my best races, I managed to refocus and finish strong, graduating the December after my last semester of eligibility.

During your final semester, or after your eligibility ends, don't let the tendency to lose focus academically make you succumb to senioritis.

REALITY CHECK:
Your grades from your first to last semester always matter and affect your overall GPA.

Even though it may be challenging, work hard on going out with a bang. This may boost not only your grades but also your self-confidence and your relationships with others, like your professors, who can help you to transition successfully into the next phase of your life.

SO YOU WANT TO TURN PRO

Most college programs aim to develop your athletic potential over the course of your eligibility. Few coaches expect freshmen to lead their teams to championship titles; most expect this from their upperclassmen. In college, you are basically in an "athletic incubator" mainly because the NCAA provides certain protections for you as a student-athlete. For example, if you receive financial aid and underperform on the field, your scholarship cannot be cut solely for this reason. In contrast, competing in the pros is strictly about business—relationships matter, but the financial bottom line usually matters more. Teams and sponsors usually want quick returns on their financial investments in you. Most of these contracts have clauses allowing them to reduce or end their financial or contractual relationships with you if your athletic performance, attitude, or conduct does not meet their standards.

REALITY CHECK:
Competing in the world of professional sports is like playing musical chairs—there are always more athletes than available jobs.

As a professional athlete, you constantly have to position yourself to get a "seat" ahead of potentially faster, stronger, hungrier, and more experienced and skilled athletes. It is literally survival of the fittest, and if you are not fit enough. then you will soon be out of a job. In other words, it's cutthroat in the pros, and you are expendable because someone else is always gunning for your position.

Being successful as a professional athlete requires more than just athletic abilities. You need to be physically, mentally, emotionally, and spiritually ready to deal with various circumstances that you may face in the pros. These include injuries, adjustments to your playing time or role on the team, contract issues, trades, demotions, or drastic changes—up or down—in your income. How you handle the pressures to perform, the media, and fans also affect the success of your pro career.

At some stage, like most athletes, you probably daydreamed about becoming a professional athlete. However, if you neglect what you should be doing as a student-athlete because you are banking your future on turning pro, then you seriously need to rethink your plan. Each year, only a small fraction of student-athletes turns pro in their sport. Those who have a real chance at making a living playing their sport professionally or semiprofessionally *consistently* put up draft-worthy and pro-compatible numbers and performances (how's your stat line?). Still there are no guarantees. Serious injuries or some unexpected circumstances, like getting into serious legal troubles, have ended many potential professional athletes' dreams and careers.

Even if you are a legitimate pro prospect, you should not treat your academics or your collegiate experience lightly. The lessons, skills, and maturity gained from trying to be the best student-athlete that you can be will serve you well in the pros and in life. Consider your readiness carefully before you make that big jump if you are not a senior, especially if you don't currently have a positive and genuine support team to give you encouragement and important reality checks so you can stay properly grounded.

REALITY CHECK:
If you lack the discipline and maturity to do well as a student-athlete in a system specifically designed to help you succeed, you will likely struggle in the pros where there are far fewer checks and balances and far more opportunities to mess up.

Bear in mind that the average professional career in some sports is relatively short. Also consider that, rather than becoming "set for life," a high number of professional athletes face financial crisis during their careers or soon after their retirement. Reasons for this include reductions or loss of contracts due to career-changing injuries, poor performances, or problematic lifestyles. Or because of lavish spending or failure to save or invest properly. Without college degrees to "fall back on," good reputations, and the right contacts, athletes' earning potential away from sports can be severely limited.

I tried to find out as much as I could about the professional world in my sport before I became a professional athlete. I recommend that you do the same *before* you bank your future on turning pro or you become a professional athlete. You may be shocked or disappointed to learn that the realities for the *average* professional athlete in your sport or playing your position are much different than you expected. Being a professional athlete is not all glitz and glam as it is often portrayed in the media. A lot more goes on—both good and bad—away from the sound bites and highlight reels.

Even if you have a good chance of being an outstanding professional athlete in your sport, this information will give you a solid perspective for your future. Take time to research potential agents or advisors thoroughly because their actions can significantly affect your reputation and your wallet, especially as a rookie. Make sure that they are reputable and professional and show a real interest in you beyond how much fame, power, or money you can bring them. Don't do anything that could harm you or your school, such as accepting illegal payments or gifts. Also be wary of "yes" people and new "friends" before and after you turn pro because their presence in your life could prove troublesome.

If possible, keep going to classes and trying to do well instead of quitting school completely after your last collegiate competition. I know this can be challenging if you are a pro prospect who must travel to tryouts or specialized training to improve your stock in the draft, but do your best. Try to leave school in good standing—academically and otherwise—so it is easier to pick up where you left off if you choose to return to school. You can do this by always being respectful toward others, developing the right relationships, particularly with your coaches, advisors, and professors, and keeping a good reputation while you are still a student-athlete. In other words, build—don't burn—bridges during your college career.

CONTINUE YOUR EDUCATION

It is smart to keep working toward your college degree even after you turn pro because you never know what the future holds. A college degree is a personal accomplishment and may open many doors for you. In fact, earning your college degree may inspire others, such as your family, friends, or fans, to elevate their lives through higher education. Use some of the money you earn to pay for school in your off-seasons instead of buying the latest cars or depreciable gadgets. You can lose your money by investing in the stock market and businesses, or it can be stolen, but you can never lose what you invest in your education.

Like many student-athletes, including me, your eligibility may finish before you earn your college degree. Try to complete your degree as soon as possible before you lose your rhythm as a student or your life circumstances and obligations become more complicated or demanding, such as having a family or relocating for work. Remember that the cost of education rises every year, so you may have to make some financial sacrifices. In addition to working at a job, you may be able to secure a student loan or grant to fund your remaining courses. The student grant approval process is often lengthy and competitive; apply early and consider getting some help so your application is done correctly and stands out. Your coaches, professors, and advisors may suggest ways for you to continue your education, such as becoming a graduate or teaching assistant. Many schools offer online or correspondence courses that may be more economical and convenient for you. Consider your options and create a feasible plan to earn your degree.

I have several friends who graduated on extended timelines, ranging from two to ten years, based on their financial and personal circumstances. Some registered for evening classes at their local community colleges, while others took online courses. A few who turned pro in their sport enrolled in classes during their off-seasons. Although it took them a while, their financial and personal sacrifices paid off. Remember, how long it takes you to earn your college degree is less important than earning that degree.

PREPARE FOR LIFE AFTER SPORTS

Transitions—big and small—are an unavoidable part of life and need proper preparation. Right now, you may be a few weeks, months, or years away from facing the moment when your time as a student-athlete ends. When that happens, you will have to make the transition to a new phase. Being competitive in sports will play a different role in your daily life, but the skills and habits that you practiced in college will transfer to your new career, whatever course it takes.

Unless you qualify to play in a professional or semi-professional league, most of your post-collegiate competitions will be recreational. Perhaps playing professional sports may make you one of the few who become financially secure for the rest of your life. Even then, you cannot postpone the unavoidable forever.

REALITY CHECK:
Although you may not want to think about it, at some point in your life your athletic career will end and you will have to live life after sports.

Of course, you may remain seriously involved in sports through coaching or administration, but the days when being a competitive athlete is central to your daily life will end someday.

Although most student-athletes accept this fact, the adjustment period can naturally seem scary. Perhaps for the first time in your life you will have to take on adult responsibilities without the daily guidance of coaches, the help of teammates, or the support of fans. This adjustment can be more difficult if you have competed in sports for most of your life or you are used to being in the spotlight. The same is true if you have finished your career with a tough loss or unfulfilled athletic dreams, if you have allowed sports to define you, or if you did not develop other interests or areas of your life.

Even though you may now have a good support system of friends and family, life after college means a significant increase in personal, legal, professional, and financial responsibilities. No athletic department-type organization exists in the real world with paid advisors to ensure that you always do what you need to do. You will be an adult, expected to conduct yourself accordingly and to make a positive contribution to society.

To become successful in life after sports you need to develop the right plans, attitudes, and tools. This means applying to your daily life many of the success principles learned from others, your experiences, and this book. Start laying the groundwork now for when you reach the end zone, so you are emotionally, psychologically, and professionally ready to face the future and win.

TIPS FOR POST-COLLEGIATE SUCCESS

- Define what success after college means for you.
- Keep working toward whatever career, lifestyle, and quality of life you want after school.
- Develop basic life skills such as setting proper goals and managing your time and money wisely as well as cooking, cleaning, and doing laundry.
- Stay proactive about taking the next steps toward your goals, whether furthering your education or seeking employment.
- Give others incentives and opportunities to "buy in" and participate in your success; create a clear plan for what you hope to accomplish and get the right people involved as early as possible.

- Build your own brand by "selling" your unique personal story, marketing your strengths, and tapping into your network.
- Don't quit, especially during tough times; use your competitiveness, skills, contacts, and experiences to your advantage.

NETWORK, NETWORK, NETWORK

Real estate agents' mantra is "location, location, location," because that is often the factor that most affects the value of a property. Networking is to personal, social, and professional advancement what location is to real estate. Networking matters. In the past, a college degree may have been enough to secure your future. In today's world, though, networking is essential to building bridges to future opportunities and relationships, and to doing well in life.

REALITY CHECK:
If you don't grow your personal,
social, and professional network, you will
fall behind in today's world.

As the saying goes, "It's not what you know, but who you know" that ultimately makes a difference in what opportunities come your way and even in how quickly you can advance in some areas. People usually prefer to interact with someone they know or someone connected to a common contact. Who you know often determines if you will get your foot in the door or get a second look. Many times, having a mutual contact or common reference, not just great qualifications and personality, can change a potential dead end into an opportunity.

You might cross paths with someone only for a semester or a few years in college, but that connection may later prove mutually beneficial. For example, a teammate today might later become a potential employer or important reference for a job and vice versa. Similarly, a classmate might become a lifelong friend or even a spouse.

Growing your network increases your opportunity base personally, socially, and professionally. Creating a useful network and using it to your advantage takes time. Your college years may be your greatest chance to grow your network and work on your networking skills. Often after you leave college, your base of new contacts shrinks to those in your immediate circles, such as your workplace, neighborhood, and religious or social organizations. Because people in these groups tend to share similar characteristics, your interactions with them will probably limit your chances of expanding your skills to grow a more diverse network. On the other hand, most colleges have people—staff and students—from different backgrounds, so you can potentially build a larger and more diverse pool of contacts.

In recent years, online social networking sites such as Facebook, MySpace, and Twitter and professional networking sites like LinkedIn have exploded onto the scene and changed how people around the world network. Most of these sites have free membership, but some require a paid subscription to join or upgrade. Registering and creating your personal or professional profile usually takes only a few minutes and gives you instant access to other members. Because many of these sites also allow you to view and connect with your contacts' contacts, you can create an extensive network. If you don't have great interpersonal skills, or you lack diversity or size in your current contact base, then online networking could boost your network portfolio and give you more exposure.

Online networking does have some risks. Because many social networking sites provide a platform for users to upload and post all kinds of content such as personal information, comments, pictures, and videos, you can easily forget that users other than your intended audience may also access this information. Because student-athletes tend to have higher profiles, you could also potentially become the target of online scammers, stalkers, rival fans, or even the media trolling the Internet looking for any information that they can use against you or your school.

Not long ago, some publicized incidents involving student-athletes prompted several schools to make policies about posting inappropriate content on the Internet, including social networking sites, blogs, and forums. These measures help student-athletes avoid situations that could potentially embarrass them, their families, and their schools and its supporters. Follow your school's policy and be careful about what content you post on the Internet, especially personal, questionable, or sensitive information. This includes writing posts criticizing your team, coaches, school, or rivals, or uploading pictures or videos that show you or others in compromising situations. Also keep in mind that those who review applications for jobs or postgraduate positions often search the Internet to get a better profile of candidates. So think about how a posting may help or hurt you or others in the future before you do it. Remember that although some content might be removable, you may be too late to repair the damage to your reputation, eligibility, personal safety, or relationships.

GET READY FOR THE WORKFORCE

Unless you inherited a fortune or have otherwise become wealthy, then at some stage you will have to work for a living.

If you have never worked, you will likely be behind the curve compared with those who have held summer jobs, done internships, or gained some other real-world work experience.

Most times before you get a chance to have a face-to-face meeting with a potential employer, you will have to submit a cover letter and résumé. If poorly written, they can quickly overshadow your credentials and sink your prospects. When possible, try to take a course that involves some form of résumé writing and job interview preparation. If you can't find such a course, talk to your academic advisor or career counselor about getting help in those areas. Many online resources offer assistance with preparing these documents, as well as provide other useful tips about interviewing techniques and researching and securing the right job.

Like a recruiting visit, a job interview will often provide the first in-person meeting between you and potential employers. Besides what they read on paper, they want to know how you will add value and fit into their organization. They will likely pose questions or scenarios to evaluate your knowledge and ethics. They will also note your demeanor, preparedness, and appearance, including your hairstyle, clothes, or whether you have prominent tattoos or piercings. Bear in mind that how you look may immediately shape their impression of you—for better or worse. Take time to develop your wardrobe, interview skills, vocabulary, and knowledge about the industry or specific company for which you are applying. First impressions matter to employers, and they should to you too. Remember that you also need to consider if working for them is right for you at that time.

Many employers, especially in jobs with much autonomy, such as sales, like to hire former athletes. Most athletes are self-motivated, can multitask, are able to work in team environments, and stay committed to working through tough times to reach goals. Selling your personal story and your strong points as a former athlete may allow you to stand out from the crowd. Being a former student-athlete could work in your favor, particularly when you lack work experience or you enter a competitive industry.

FIND THE RIGHT JOB FOR YOU

What is the right job for you? There is no simple answer, but it will likely provide enjoyment, as well as personal, professional, and financial rewards. It will also fit your values and allow you to develop and maximize your skills. Perhaps you were thinking more about one where you can work fewer than ten hours a week—from your yacht, of course—earn an outrageous tax-free salary, and enjoy an eleven-month vacation every year. Now, let's get back to reality!

Although everyone wants that high-paying, low-stress job straight out of college, sometimes, regardless of your credentials or contacts, you just have to get your feet wet and "pay dues" before you can find a position with more perks and more money. You may have to take a less than ideal job in order to start paying off outstanding student loans or other significant financial obligations, like your rent or car loan. These temporary realities should not deter you from continuing to develop your skills and seeking some form of job advancement. For example, my father packed boxes at a local department store while working on his master's degree, but he did not lose sight of his goal. The money he earned allowed him to finish his degree, which later helped him become a university professor.

Many factors contribute to how quickly you find the job that is right for you, including the school you attended, your credentials—education, grades, work experience—who you know, the competitiveness of the field, and the current economic climate. Visit with your academic advisor or career counselor for guidance and resource materials to get you started. Talking with your professors may give you useful contacts or ideas about the best steps for entering a specific field of work. These people are usually also good references on your résumé, so try to keep them in your corner.

Career services centers at most schools host career fairs for their students. Attending these fairs is a great way to build your professional network, understand the current marketplace, and put your résumé into the hands of potential employers. Also consider using job recruiters, headhunters, and employment agencies, which can offer helpful tips and links to employers. The Internet can also be a powerful tool for research and interaction with potential employers. For instance, many companies post employment opportunities on their websites and encourage applicants to e-mail their résumés directly to them. You can access many of these options right now at little or no cost. Even if you are months or years away from entering the workforce, start now to familiarize yourself with trends in the marketplace and the job search process. This information can be especially useful if you have not yet declared a major.

Start thinking about and getting ready for life after sports. When your time as a student-athlete comes to an end, you will face a big transition. How well you handle this transition will often affect you personally, socially, professionally, and financially for a long time. I am confident that if you use your resources, skills, and the suggestions and reality checks in this book, you will do well both now and in the future. The world is yours.

ONE-ON-ONE

- What does it take to become a professional athlete in your sport? How do your stat line and readiness compare with the pros'?

- What goals and "game plans" do you have for your life after college and after sports?

- How diverse is your current network and how good are your networking skills? What can you do to improve both?

- What can you do to get ready for the workforce?

- What life skills are you developing? What others do you need to work on?

REALITY CHECK: "SECRETS" OF A CHAMPION STUDENT-ATHLETE

- Your degree of commitment determines your success. Your time in college serves as your training ground for personal, athletic, and professional development. You can pursue both your sports and academic goals at a high level.

- Encounters with new people, situations, and ideas will challenge you in some ways. Take time now to know who you are and what you want as a student, as an athlete, and as a person. Stay true to yourself but also take full advantage of opportunities to become better in these areas of your life.

- Learn and follow the rules—written, spoken, and unspoken. You can learn most rules by reading, observing, and asking questions. Use the rules to help you understand and master the "game."

- Being proactive allows you to take greater control of your life because you are constantly involved in how it unfolds. Take the initiative in going after your goals by planning, accessing your resources, and getting the right people involved to help you. Follow through until the end.

- Develop a personal system or "game plan" that works best for you instead of randomly approaching your studies, athletics, and other situations. Your skills and performances will improve and become more consistent when you do.

- Setting and working toward personal goals are important keys to success in sports and life. Proper goals give you direction and help you to focus your resources and energy better. Without goals, you fail to live up to your potential, and you can fall prey to distractions and mediocrity. When you align your goals with your core values, your journey becomes easier.

- When you control your time, you control your success. Every moment of every day as a student-athlete is valuable and irreplaceable. The sooner you learn how to make every second count, the more success you will enjoy. Keep track of your "game clock" as a student-athlete.

- How much stress you have and how you handle it affect your life in many ways. Your lifestyle plays a significant role in your success in the classroom and on the field. Control your social life or it can ruin you. As a student-athlete, your body is perhaps your biggest asset. Treat it with respect and give yourself the greatest chance to perform at your best.

- Your academics always matter and should always be a top priority. Use your competitiveness, creativity, and any available resources to do well in the classroom.

Learn to treat your classes like "games" and get your academic advisors and instructors on your "team" early.

- Champions feel like winners before they lace up to compete. Your preparation and the skills you use against your opponents determine how well you perform and if you will win. Developing a champion mind-set allows you to prepare thoroughly to execute best when it matters most.

- Beside academic and athletic development, your college experience provides a great foundation for your future. Use the opportunity that you have to interact with many different people to grow your network, build your brand, and prepare for the workforce.

Finally, remember that knowledge has no end—there's so much more to learn beyond your textbooks and your playbook, especially after you graduate. Stay in touch with the real world of political, economic, and social affairs around you right now so that you can be up to date and competitive whatever you choose to do in college and beyond. Appreciate those who care enough to give you encouragement and frequent reality checks. Your time as a student-athlete will pass quickly, so enjoy this incredible journey and make the most of it.

About the Author

When Obadele Thompson left his home and family in Barbados to travel almost 3,000 miles to attend college, he faced the challenges of balancing being a student and an athlete. His journey to the Olympic podium led him through all the trials and triumphs that still face collegiate athletes. Through these challenges, family, mentors, coaches, and friends served as "reality checks" that helped guide him to achieve his best—in the classroom and in competition. In *Secrets of a Champion Student-Athlete,* he shares what he learned along the way and offers his version of "A Reality Check" for current and future students who are also athletes.

By the time he graduated from The University of Texas-El Paso (UTEP), he had won four individual NCAA titles and set two NCAA records (one still stands). He ranked in the Top 5 in the world in the 200-meter dash in his junior and senior years and established three World Records: the World Junior Record in the 100-meter dash as a freshman, the fastest 100-meter dash under any conditions (a time which stood for 12 years) in his junior season, and the 55-meter dash in his senior year. He finished as an 11-time NCAA All-American and 16-time Western Athletic Conference (WAC) Champion who co-captained his team to back-to-back Conference Championships. He also won the NCAA Indoor Athlete of the Year Award in track and field and the WAC Student-Athlete of the Year Award. To cap his collegiate career, he was honored with one of the NCAA's highest awards for student-athletes: the Today's Top VIII Award.

He excelled in his academic career by being named to the Dean's List four times, honored as a WAC Academic All-American, and designated a GTE First Team-At-Large Academic All-American. Inducted into the Beta Gamma Sigma international honor society for top business students, he graduated Summa Cum Laude in Economics and Marketing, also collecting the UTEP Top Ten Senior Award.

For over a decade after his graduation, he continued among the world's top-rated sprinters, traveling to over thirty countries and participating in three Olympic Games and seven World Championships. He reached his highest IAAF World Rankings of #3 in the 100m dash (2000) and #1 in the 200m dash (2001). In the 2000 Olympic Games in Sydney, he won his country's first individual Olympic medal by placing third in the 100m dash.

"Oba" continues sharing his reality checks and guiding student-athletes as a speaker, mentor, consultant, and author. He has been featured in *The New York Times* and *USA Today*. After he won his historic medal, his former Prime Minister appointed him Ambassador and Special Envoy of the Youth of Barbados. Oba passionately shares his belief that everyone can enjoy success through principled living.

Obadele Thompson lives in Austin, Texas, with his wife, Marion Jones, and their three children. His definition of "champion" now extends to being a father.